HOW TO PRAY ALWAYS
(Without Always Praying)

Silvio E. Fittipaldi

LIGUORI
PUBLICATIONS

One Liguori Drive
Liguori, Missouri 63057
(314) 464-2500

Imprimi Potest:
John F. Dowd, C.SS.R.
Provincial, St. Louis Province
Redemptorist Fathers

Imprimatur:
+ Edward J. O'Donnell
Vicar General, Archdiocese of St. Louis

ISBN 0-89243-237-3
Library of Congress Catalog Card Number: 85-80599

Excerpts from THE JERUSALEM BIBLE, copyright © 1966 by Darton, Longman & Todd, Ltd. and Doubleday & Company, Inc. Reprinted by permission of the publisher.

Excerpts from TALES OF THE HASIDIM, The Early Masters, Vol. II, by Martin Buber, copyright © 1947, by Schocken Books, Inc. Reprinted by permission of Schocken Books, Inc.

Excerpts from THE WAY OF CHUANG TZU, by Thomas Merton, copyright © 1965 by The Abbey of Gethsemani, Inc. Reprinted by permission of New Directions Publishing Corporation.

Four (4) lines of poetry from ZEN: POEMS, PRAYERS, SERMONS, ANECDOTES, INTERVIEWS, translated by Lucien Stryk and Takoshi Ikemoto, 1981. Reprinted with the permission of Ohio University Press/Swallow Press.

Excerpts from ZEN BUDDHISM AND PSYCHOANALYSIS, by Erich Fromm, D. T. Suzuki, and R. DeMartino, copyright © 1960 by Erich Fromm. Reprinted by permission of Harper & Row Publishers, Inc.

Cover by Pam Hummelsheim

The scene on the cover was drawn by Dr. Frederick Franck, in the Imperial Palace Gardens, Kyoto. Frederick Franck's drawings and paintings form part of the permanent collections of the Museum of Modern Art, the Fogg Museum, and the Tokyo National Museum.

Contents

Contents

Introduction
What Is Prayer, Anyway?

Saint Paul has recommended: "Pray always." But in our technological society, it would seem that we have forgotten how to pray.

Or have we?

The reality of prayer is often viewed in a narrow way. Some people think of it only in terms of verbal formulas and community worship services or as communication with God or as work. And these concepts of prayer are often experienced as falling short of Paul's recommendation to pray "always."

In this book I do not propose that the above concepts of prayer are incorrect. Rather, it is my purpose to broaden the *concept* of prayer so that the *reality* of it may be more fully recognized.

The thesis on which this book is based is the following:

Prayer is a human reality. It is grounded in, and is a realization of, human experiences.

These experiences have been formalized in an effort to teach human persons to pray and, by praying, to realize their humanity more fully.

To realize the reality of the forms of prayer, one must get behind these forms and make contact with the experiences they express. The forms point to the experiences.

By getting behind the forms to the experiences, the "always" of "Pray always" may become realizable. Prayer, then, would not be so much something that is done. Rather, prayerfulness would be an orientation in life.

The experience of prayer has human roots. Some of these roots that will be discussed in this book are: *Questioning; Wonder; Silence; Concentration; Relatedness; Perceptiveness; Grace; and Wisdom.*

This book, in many ways, is not simply the result of my own experience and reflection. I am deeply indebted to my many friends and teachers who have shared their lives and their questions and their answers with me. While their thinking may rise to the surface on many of the following pages, I take full responsibility for what is said. Furthermore, while I am committed within the Christian tradition, I have been greatly influenced by the other major religious traditions in the world. The following pages are an attempt to articulate an experience of prayer which crosses over the boundaries of the religious traditions as I have assimilated and integrated them into my vision of life.

Finally, I would like to dedicate this book to my parents, Edward and Elvira Fittipaldi, who have given me life and continue to support me; and to Reverend John A. Klekotka, O.S.A., who has encouraged me in many ways during the past dozen years, both actively and by his very being.

1

Speaking About Prayer

The Way to Prayer

In California, on his way to the Orient a few months before he died, Thomas Merton was asked to speak about prayer. He replied:

> Nothing that anyone says will be that important. The
> great thing is prayer. Prayer itself. If you want a life
> of prayer, the way to get it is by praying.

Merton was saying something very important about the overconceptualizing that takes place when prayer is spoken of.

During the last ten years or so of his life, Merton was deeply influenced by the spirituality of the Orient, especially that of Zen. And one of the basic concerns of Zen is with an over-intellectualizing of life. In our time people have benefited much from science, and scientific method has become an idol. This method involves much analyzing of data, breaking down a whole and doing a thorough investigation of it. At the root of this method, in the popular imagination, is an impeccable logic. It is thought that if something is logical, then it is true. Our language, and hence our speech, is an expression of that logic — which is a thing of the mind.

In Zen there is a saying: "Not relying on words or letters." This saying is thought to express one dimension of the essence of Zen. It does not deny intellection or language or words or speech. Rather, it points to what is at the root of speech, what is prior to speech. "Prior" here does not mean prior in terms of time but in what might be called an ontological sense. Shin'ichi Hisamatsu, a contemporary Zen Buddhist, suggests that "not relying on words or letters" is to be "taken to mean 'prior to words' in the sense of not depending on words, not being bound or caught by words."[1] The words point to something beyond themselves.

From a Christian point of view, this is expressed in the Gospel According to John where Jesus says:

> You study the scriptures,
> believing that in them you have eternal life;
> now these same scriptures testify to me,
> and yet you refuse to come to me for life!
> (John 5:39-40)

Neither the Zen saying nor the saying attributed to Jesus condemns speech or words or study or concepts. Both point to the root of these articulations.

Often, we get so wrapped up in our concepts or our language that we forget to live. We forget the very thing we are talking about. So, too, in speech about prayer, we may become so engrossed in the beautiful descriptions of prayer that we might forget the experience they are attempting to communicate. Thus Merton can say: "If you want a life of prayer, the way to get it is by praying."

Limits and Power of Language

A second aspect of Merton's statement is that it points to the inherent limitation of words. When a word is spoken, something is said — but not everything is said. This is deftly pointed out in a story told by a great Chinese sage, Chuang Tzu. Before he tells the story, Chuang Tzu discusses the value of books:

> The world values books, and thinks that in so doing it is valuing life. But books contain words only. And yet there is something else which gives value to the books. Not the words only, not the thought in the words, but something else within the thought, swinging it in a certain direction that words cannot apprehend. But it is the words themselves that the world values when it commits them to books; and though the world values them, these words are worthless as long as that which gives them value is not held in honor. That which man apprehends by observation is only outward form and color, name and noise; and he thinks that this will put him in possession of Life. Form and color, name and sound, do not reach to reality. That is why: "He who knows does not say; he who says, does not know."[2]

An inherent paradox is involved in this saying. I might ask the author or speaker why he even said what he said if "he who says does not know." Is it then true that *he* does not know and that, hence, his words can be doubted? The question is asked: "How then is the world going to know Life through words?" In response, Chuang Tzu tells the following story about Duke Hwan and the wheelwright:

> Duke Hwan of Khi, first in his dynasty, sat under his canopy reading his philosophy; and Phien, the wheelwright, was out in the yard making a wheel. Phien laid aside hammer and chisel, climbed the steps, and said to Duke Hwan: "May I ask you,

9

Lord, what is this you are reading?" The Duke said: "The experts. The authorities." And Phien asked: "Are they alive or dead?" "Dead a long time," was the reply. "Then," said the wheelwright, "you are reading only the dirt they left behind." Then the Duke replied: "What do you know about it? You are only a wheelwright. You had better give me a good explanation or else you must die." The wheelwright said: "Let us look at the affair from my point of view. When I make wheels, if I go easy, they fall apart; if I am too rough, they do not fit. If I am neither too easy nor too violent, they come out right. The work is what I want it to be. You cannot put this into words; you have to know how it is. I cannot even tell my own son exactly how it is done, and my son cannot learn it from me. So here I am seventy years old, still making wheels! The men of old took all they really knew with them to the grave. And so, Lord, what you are reading there is only the dirt they left behind them."[3]

Yet, words also have a power to them. Not only do they conceal, they also reveal. And in revealing, they can heal. A word spoken at the right moment, at the right place, to the right person! What power! Thus, there is within the great religious traditions of the world a recognition of the force of words, of speech. This is more evident in Judaism, Christianity, and Islam which are known as religions of the word. The Scriptures of these traditions are deeply honored and studied. It is the wise person, however, who not only studies the Scriptures but also lives them. Or better, the Scriptures give expression to the life of the wise person. For "the fool says what he knows; the wise man knows what he says," suggests the Hasidic Master, Rabbi Bunam.[4] Or, as Bernard Phillips, one of my teachers, once said in class: "The wise man may not know the Scriptures. But if they are repeated to him, it is he who can point to their deepest meaning.''

Related Speech

The power of speech is not only recognized by the Near-Eastern religions — Judaism, Christianity, and Islam. It is also recognized by Buddhism. One of the elements of the Buddhist Noble Eightfold Path — an expression of the Enlightenment of the Buddha — is ''Right Speech.'' Right Speech does not refer exclusively to speaking the truth or not lying, though this is included. Right Speech means related speech: real communication, which may take place during dialogue. It does not necessarily take place in that setting; the parties may be speaking past each other. Nor is it excluded from a ''lecture.'' Real communication takes place when the words move from heart to heart, from mind to mind, from person to person. The words do not come solely from the one speaking but also from the one being spoken to. This is related speech. A good example of such speech is found in an Hasidic story:

> Every evening after prayer, the Baal-Shem went to his room. Two candles were set in front of him and the mysterious Book of Creation put on the table among other books. Then all those who needed his counsel were admitted in a body, and he spoke with them until the eleventh hour. One evening, when the people left, one of them said to the man beside him how much good the words the Baal-Shem had directed to him had done him. But the other told him not to talk such nonsense, that they had entered the room together and from that moment on the master had spoken to no one except himself. A third, who heard this, joined in the conversation with a smile, saying how curious that both were mistaken, for the

11

rabbi had carried on an intimate conversation with him the entire evening. Then a fourth and a fifth made the same claim, and finally all began to talk at once and tell what they had experienced. But the next instant they all fell silent.[5]

Related speech is speech which is spoken from the heart of one to another in such a way that it comes from the very heart of the listener, yet it still comes from the one speaking. The speaker really speaks. Why? The speaker knows what is said and says what is known.

In his first Letter to the Corinthians, Saint Paul speaks of the gift of tongues. He advises that this gift be for the benefit of the community, that it be related to the members of the community. He asks:

> . . . what use shall I be if all my talking reveals nothing new, tells you nothing, and neither inspires you nor instructs you? . . . There are any number of different languages in the world, and not one of them is meaningless, but if I am ignorant of what the sounds mean, I am a savage to the man who is speaking, and he is a savage to me. (1 Corinthians 14:6,10-11)

Paul is concerned with whether or not his speech is related speech.

Prayer

This, too, can be said of speech about prayer: it is quite limited. It is the dirt that is left behind. It is that which points and should not be confused with what it points to. Yet, it is also powerful. It does point. Hence, it can be healing, enlightening, instructive, and creative. We read in the Book of Genesis:

God *said*, "Let there be light," and there was light.
(Genesis 1:3)

And John the Evangelist proclaimed:

> In the beginning was the Word:
> The Word was with God
> and the Word was God. (John 1:1)

And this Word can make us free:

> If you make my word your home
> you will indeed be my disciples,
> you will learn the truth
> and the truth will make you free. (John 8:31-32)

Our question, then, is not whether one can speak about prayer. The question is: Who is the one who is speaking?

The Book of Sirach describes this person in terms of silence and speech:

> There is the man who keeps quiet and is considered
> wise,
> another incurs hatred for talking too much.
> There is the man who keeps quiet, not knowing how
> to answer,
> another keeps quiet, because he knows when to
> speak.
> A wise man will keep quiet till the right moment,
> but a garrulous fool will always misjudge it.
>
> The man who talks too much will get himself
> disliked,
> and the self-appointed oracle will make himself
> hated. (Sirach 20:5-8)

Words and speech both reveal and conceal. And both revealing and concealing can happen because of the hearer or the speaker. When the speaker speaks from the heart, the words reveal. But they may not be heard by the hearer. Jesus once said: "Let him who has ears to hear, hear." The hearer must also allow the heart to enter the words of the speaker.

On the other hand, the words of the speaker may conceal. They may be words to which the speaker is unrelated. Yet, it might happen that the hearer may hear. The words may speak to the hearer. The heart of the hearer is in the words. Thus, to speak about prayer or to read or hear about prayer is to put one's heart into the words. Then the words take on flesh, the flesh of the speaker and/or the hearer.

Speech about prayer, finally, is closely interwoven with one's attitude toward God — toward who this God is. I do not wish to go into my own beliefs in this matter at any great length. (To some extent my beliefs will come through what I say of prayer.) I simply will give expression to my general approach to God.

The word *God* is the best word we have for saying what we want to say, Karl Rahner suggests in one of his talks, because it tells us nothing.[6] In other words, God is ineffable, the infinite horizon and ultimate depth of life itself. God is mystery. By mystery I do not mean that nothing can be known. Rather, something is known, but we can always know more. We human persons, insofar as we are made in the "image of God," are also mystery and, hence, an imageless image. Thus, I suggest that speech about prayer is speech about God and about the human person. It is about God as Other and about God as nearer to us than we are to ourselves. And it is about the human person as that being who, as Karl Rahner suggests, is "inescapably thrust out of himself into that absolute mystery which is called God" or as "that being which loses itself in God."[7]

When we "understand" God in this way, prayer is not only a communication between God and human persons; it goes beyond that to being a *communion* of God and human beings. To speak of prayer is to speak of God and of human persons and of their communion. Insofar as this speech is about mystery (and possibly arises out of mystery), it both reveals and conceals. Something is said, but not everything.

Finally, I would like to suggest that speech about prayer can itself be prayer. It can be a way of entering into the mystery of God and human beings and the world. When it comes from the heart, speech about prayer is a participation in this mystery, a living of this mystery, a being grasped by this mystery.

Notes

1. Shin'ichi Hisamatsu, "Zen: Its Meaning for Modern Civilization," *The Eastern Buddhist,* New Series 1 (September, 1965), p. 23.
2. Thomas Merton, *The Way of Chuang Tzu* (New York: New Directions, 1965), p. 82.
3. Ibid., pp. 82-83.
4. Martin Buber, *Tales of the Hasidim: The Later Masters* (New York: Schocken, 1948), p. 256.
5. Martin Buber, *Tales of the Hasidim: The Early Masters* (New York: Schocken, 1947), p. 55.
6. Karl Rahner, *Grace in Freedom* (New York: Herder and Herder, 1969), p. 185.
7. Karl Rahner, "Christian Humanism," *Journal of Ecumenical Studies* 4, 3 (Summer, 1967), p. 373.

2

Prayer as Questioning

Questions of the Heart

If it is true that God and human persons are mystery, then more can always be said about the mystery. Hence, anything that is said is open to question.

My use of the word *question* in this chapter is not the normal usage. Today a question is usually understood as an intellectual query. I do not wish to exclude this meaning, but I want to broaden it to include "experiential" questions. An "experiential" question is one that is asked with one's mind and heart, body and feelings, wonderings and longings. It is a question spoken not only in word but also in one's eyes and hands, ears and feet. It is a question that may be articulated, yet is very often unable to be spoken. It is the question that is contained in expectation and anticipation, in fear and in terror, in love and in hate.

Some examples may help in understanding what I mean by an "experiential" question. Imagine that someone has said to you: "I want to see you." Your mind begins to operate, wondering what the meeting is for. Emotions of fear, maybe, or even joyful expectation arise, depending on your relationship with the person. What question are you asking? You are asking this:

"Why do you want to see me?" But your question is not necessarily a spoken one. Nor is it simply mental. You feel as well as think it.

Other examples are:

"Can I trust you?" or

"Why should I get up this morning?" or

"Why don't I trust you?" or

"Can I open myself to this person?" or

"What will I do with my life?" or

"Can I keep living this way without destroying myself?" or

"Will I be able to fulfill this responsibility?" or

"What must I do — here — now?" or

"What do I really want?" or

"Will I be able to get to sleep tonight?"

These questions are not only intellectual, they are physical and emotional and relational as well.

Questions such as these are asked by different people in many different ways. They are also asked by the same person in a variety of ways. Our questions do not concern only ourselves; they may concern other people whose lives are tied to our own or even people who are strangers. Thus, we might ask:

"Will this child ever grow up and be independent?"

"Why does this elderly grandmother (or grandfather) have to suffer so much?"

At two A.M. a child coughing: "Will she ever stop coughing?"

"When will this baby stop crying?"

"What can I do to enable this child to grow?"

Self-Questioning

In *Hatter Fox*, a powerfully sensitive novel by Marilyn Harris, one of the central characters is Doctor Teague Summer. Summer is a man whose life has become a living question. He had been called to a jail in Santa Fe to care for a young man who

17

was wounded. In the same cell with the young man were twenty other inmates, male and female. One of the inmates, named Hatter Fox, attacked Summer and stabbed him in the back. During the weeks that followed, Summer was haunted by Hatter Fox. He was strangely drawn to her, and he wondered why. Finally, he went to see her. While viewing her almost lifeless body and spirit in the cell, he cried out to himself:

> Why? Why everything? Why the need for such a room? Why the need for emergency calls to jail cells where kids have cut their wrists? Why Hatter Fox? Why the human waste beyond redemption, beyond help? And finally, why in the hell was I standing there, apparently transfixed by a young girl who had tried to kill me?[1]

Summer was questioning the situation the way people question their own situation or question an event reported on the evening news. Summer was also questioning himself. He felt that he was a second-rate doctor. He had no real interest in Hatter Fox nor in her people, the Navahos. Yet, here he was in her cell. And a few days later, he would be driving to a reformatory in Albuquerque to be consulted in regard to Hatter. Summer's mind continued to spin, trying to make sense of his actions. He imagined himself as an "army-surplus Don Quixote." He felt he was a "sucker." And, finally, he could not imagine himself as anyone or anything. Hatter, it seemed, had become for him a symbol of all his past failures.

These are the questions that drove this one man — questions about himself, about others, and about the conditions in a particular place in the world. It is these questions that he lives and embodies throughout the novel.

Thomas Merton gives expression to Summer's kind of questions and to "prayer as questioning" when he writes in his book *Contemplative Prayer:*

But underlying all life is the ground of doubt and self-questioning which sooner or later must bring us face to face with the ultimate meaning of our life. This self-questioning can never be without a certain existential "dread" — a sense of insecurity, of "lostness," of exile, of sin. A sense that one has somehow been untrue not so much to abstract moral or social norms but to one's own inmost truth.[2]

Doctor Teague Summer was confronting his past failures, trying to free himself not from their reality but from their power to define him. He was in search of his own inmost truth.

God in Our Questioning

What do these questions have to do with prayer? I hope to show that they have everything to do with it.

In his personal memoir *Night*, Elie Wiesel asked the question: "Why did I pray?" He received a response from his teacher Moshe, who said:

Man raises himself toward God by the questions he asks him. . . . That is true dialogue. Man questions God and God answers. But we don't understand his answers. We can't understand them, because they come from the depths of the soul, and they stay there until death. . . . I pray to the God within me that he will give me the strength to ask him the right questions.[3]

But what does God have to do with questions like "Can I trust you?" or "When will this baby stop crying?" Questions like these do not even have God in mind. They are totally human, simple cries arising out of human situations.

And what does God have to do with the questions of Teague Summer? They do not refer to God at all. How can these questions raise a person to God, as Elie Wiesel suggests? Why even want to be raised to God?

A response to these questions (a response that is not an answer) is this: a question asked is an opening of one's self. When I ask a question, I open myself to something "other" than the usual and even "other" than myself. To ask a question is to realize that I have some input into that very situation in which the question is posed.

For example, a child gets hit in the mouth by a hockey stick. Now that this has happened, all my plans for the next few hours or even days will have to be changed. In responding to the child, I am putting something into the situation, and my input changes the situation a little.

I have been open to something other than I had planned. I have also responded and entered into that otherness. In every question, "otherness" enters into the life of the questioner. This is what it means to live life as mystery. It is an openness to unexpected otherness. But it is also the attempt to live with expected otherness, for example, to live with people who are known to be very different. This is how a person is raised toward God by the questions that are asked. The person becomes open to otherness and responds to that otherness.

However, God is not present in the questions only because the questions are openings to otherness. Questions are also expressions of a search into the depth of reality. In *Hatter Fox,* Dr. Summer questioned himself and his situation, and these questions led him deeper into the depths. The deeper he went, the closer to mystery he came, the nearer to himself and his situation. He was led to be nearer to himself than he had ever been.

As a person approaches that mystery of himself or herself, the person approaches God. By the questions he or she asks, the person continuously encounters not only otherness but the depths of nearness. God is totally other, yet nearer to us than we are to ourselves.

We do not ask questions only for the sake of conversation or to make an impression. Our questions arise from our living experience. Elie Wiesel did not ask: "What is prayer?" He asked: "Why did I pray?" Moshe's response was that he prayed because of the questions he asked; these questions were the springboard by which Elie Wiesel could raise himself up to God.

These very questions themselves are a prayer. They are a searching, a questing. (Notice how the word *quest* has the same root as the word *question*.)

Thomas Merton describes this searching questioning as characteristic of religious meditation. Merton suggests that the *search* for truth which springs from a relationship of love is a distinctive characteristic of religious meditation. This grounding in love makes our quest for truth a prayer that shatters the dark clouds standing between us and God.[4]

The truth that is sought here is the truth contained, as it were, in questions like the ones asked above: "Can I trust you?" or "What will I do with my life?" Religious meditation is not the norm for questioning; it is a formal way of trying to question in the same way we do in everyday situations. Religious meditation is a discipline by which we can become trained to ask everyday questions with our whole selves. This way of questioning is "primitive" prayer — primitive not in the sense of being immature but in the sense of being primary or basic to one's situation in life.

Elie Wiesel also said that the questions would be answered but that we would not understand the answers. However, in his novel *A Beggar in Jerusalem,* Wiesel takes this observation a little further. In this novel he is still searching for an answer. The thing to remember here is that Elie Wiesel is a Jew and has lived through a Nazi concentration camp, an experience that shattered him. He writes:

Once, in the Orient, I talked of suicide with a sage whose clear and gentle eyes seemed forever to be gazing at a never-ending sunset. "Dying is no solution," he affirmed. "And living?" I asked. "Nor living either," he conceded. "But who tells you there is a solution?"

You will not convince me he was not right. He was too wise not to realize that one can do without solutions. Only the questions matter. We may share them or turn away from them. Either way, you will in the end admit they hold no answers. Only secrets.[5]

Many people continue to seek solutions. Is God the solution? Is God the answer to my questions? A positive response to this question may have many meanings. It may mean that I can see no light anywhere, but that I have to believe there is some answer or I can't keep going.

It may be a cop-out, where God becomes the solution, where God fills up the blanks in our knowledge.

Or, it may mean merely that the answer is not yet evident, but that I trust I will someday, somehow find an answer.

Is Jesus the answer? The same can be said for Jesus as for God.

Then is love the answer? Wiesel responds to this question, perhaps responding also to the question whether or not God is the answer. He writes: "Do you understand now that love, no matter how personal or universal, is not a solution? And that outside of love there is no solution."[6]

Love does not tell me what I must do. Questions arise and are answered in a dialogue of love. More questions arise from the answers, and so on. I am reminded here of the delightful Sufi tale concerning Nasrudin. One day Nasrudin was asked: "Why do you always answer a question with another question?" Immediately, Nasrudin responded: "Do I?"[7]

22

Questioning — A Way of Life

To have a question answered by another question that is answered by a further question can become somewhat unnerving. This path is not the easiest, and Wiesel is very aware of this. In his novel *The Town Beyond the Wall*, he writes:

> It isn't easy to live always under a question mark. But who says that the essential question has an answer? The essence of man is to be a question, and the essence of the question is to be without answer.[8]

To live under a question, especially one without answer, is truly not an easy path to follow. The difficulty is also evident in Jnana Yoga, the Way of Knowledge. Among the Hindus, the Way of Knowledge is the path to liberation for those who have a strong "intellectual" bent. It is the shortest path, but also the steepest. The spirit of this way is expressed by the Jewish prophet Jeremiah, who placed the following words on the tongue of Yahweh:

> Then when you call to me, and come to plead with me, I will listen to you. When you seek me you shall find me, when you seek me with all your heart; I will let you find me. . . . (Jeremiah 29:12-14)

The way is called the Way of Knowledge, but the "knowledge" is the knowledge of the heart, where "heart" symbolizes the core of a person. This is the way of pleading and seeking, the way of questioning. It is further illustrated by this story told to me by Bernard Phillips:

A Hindu guru and his disciple were traveling from village to village. They walked for several hours during which time they were in deep conversation concerning fundamental questions of life and God. They came upon a river. The guru stopped, guided his disciple to the river, and proceeded to hold the disciple's head under the water. He held it there until the disciple began to shake from the inability to breathe. His whole body was calling out for air. Finally, the guru allowed the disciple to come up for air. Raising his head out of the water, the disciple gasped for his breath, for his life. When he finally became calm, he asked his guru, "Why?" The guru responded: "When you want God as much as you wanted air, you will have him."

The way of questioning is certainly not an easy way, especially if the questioner cannot even expect an answer to the question. But we can also ask whether there is really a question if there is no answer.

A few years ago, I was asked by a friend what it meant to be human. The only response I could think of at the time was: "The fact that you ask that question is what it means to be human." I would add now that this is what it means to pray. To pray means to go below the surface of life. It means to live from one's depth, without losing touch with the surface of life. What takes place at the surface has depth at its heart, and one can live truly at the surface by living from that depth.

This kind of living takes trust, a trust that can be expressed in questions which attempt to enter the mystery we call life, the mystery which arises from another person, the mystery which calls to us in particular situations. To ask a question is to trust that there may be a response. To ask a question is to open oneself and, hence, to become vulnerable.

The trust is not necessarily easy. It may come forth in fear and trembling as the question of a mother and father who wonder whether their child will be able to live happily or even make a decent life in this world. Or, it may come in the question of parents who wonder whether they will have the energy to raise their disabled or disturbed child.

Such an enterprise requires trust. But this needed trust is present in a question, for the very ground of questioning is trust.

There is, however, some untrust in a question. A question can arise because of a kind of itch, an itch that all is not as it can be. If all is not as it can be, there is some mistrust of the present condition. To trust a situation totally would mean to leave it as it is. Not to trust it is to want it changed. Thus, a question contains a degree of trust that the condition can change. It also contains a mistrust of the present condition — mistrust which is a catalyst for a possible change. Prayer as this kind of questioning is grounded in trust which also has an element of mistrust.

Becoming One's Own Question

The method of questioning is deeply embedded in the traditional training of the Zen postulant. When the postulant seeks admittance to a monastery, he or she is refused at first, and is left to wait and continue seeking admittance. Upon admittance, the postulant begins the training, which is the *mondo* (question and answer). The *mondo* is one of the most characteristic features of the Zen way of teaching. This *mondo* takes place between a master and the disciple. It is the master's attempt to get the disciple to face self in all its nakedness so that enlightenment might ensue. It is the master's attempt to get the student to become the question. For, as D. T. Suzuki suggests:

> So long as the Buddha had his question before him,
> so long as he had it outside and separate from
> himself, as if it could be solved by external means, it
> could never be solved. The question comes out of the
> questioner. But when it is out, the questioner mis-
> takenly thinks it is something outside himself. The
> question is answered only when it is identified with
> the questioner.[9]

This observation by Suzuki can be illustrated by a story. There was a man who came to study under a Zen master and spent some three years of hard work in his attempt to attain enlightenment. The time was growing short until he would have to return home, so he approached the master and told him of his predicament. The master asked him to stay for two more weeks. At the end of that time, the disciple was promised, he would be enlightened. The disciple stayed the two weeks, but his state remained the same. He again approached the master who gave him another two weeks. The result was the same. The time was then reduced to five days and then to three days. The disciple was becoming anxious. He had worked hard, and there were no results. He had to go home. Still, no enlightenment. Finally, the master said to him: "Stay for three more days. If you are not enlightened by the end of that time, you will die." Within those three days the disciple was enlightened. The question was no longer outside him. He was the question.

One might get the impression that Zen *mondo* training is to be found only by encountering a human master in a Zen monastery. I suggest that for most people, who will never meet a "master," the *mondo* are provided by life itself. If our eyes and ears are open, we do not have to look beyond our own doorstep for questions. Then we could again apply Suzuki's comment: "The question is answered only when it is identified with the questioner."

Questions of the Heart in Scripture

The Christian Gospels are also sprinkled with these *mondo*-type exchanges between Jesus and his disciples or between Jesus and the leaders of the people. Since there are too many to mention here, I will point to only two.

We are all familiar with the encounter between Jesus and the Jewish doctors of the Law. At the age of twelve, when his parents took him to Jerusalem for the feast of the Passover, Jesus remained behind. When his parents found him, he was "sitting among the doctors, listening to them, and asking them questions." When Jesus was discovered, Joseph and Mary were overcome and Mary asked him: "My child, why have you done this to us? See how worried your father and I have been, looking for you."

Jesus' reply was even more significant than the fact that he was sitting and questioning the doctors of the Law. He responded to his parents with two further questions: "Why were you looking for me? . . . Did you not know that I must be busy with my Father's affairs?" (Luke 2:46,48-49)

This story is filled with questions. Most of the emphasis is usually given to Jesus' own questions, his questions to the doctors of the Law and his questions to his parents. Yet, there are times when I am more deeply touched by the profoundly human question of Mary: the question that forced her to retrace her steps to seek her only Son, who was lost; the question that came out of her body and mind and feelings; the question that welled up in her heart. Mary had truly *become* her question. It had become her prayer.

A second example is from the Gospel According to John (4:5-42). This passage describes the encounter between Jesus and the Samaritan woman at the well. This woman had persisted with her questions to Jesus, whom she recognized as a prophet. Her questions and Jesus' responses led to faith for herself and for the people of her village. Their prayer was heard. For they became their question and it became their prayer.

The *mondo* is not only a method for teaching how to pray; the *mondo* itself is the prayer. The incident with the Samaritan woman shows that questions give expression to a hidden dimension of a person or of the world. It also shows that questions can be revelatory. When we become our question, we become open to unknown responses. The response, when it comes, if it does come, may reveal to us an aspect of our being never dreamed of.

It is of the essence of a human person to be a question, and each person is made in the "image of God." This means that God, too, is a question. The "image of God" as a question is quite prominent in the prophet Hosea. The relationship of Israel to their God is portrayed as the relationship between wife and husband. The wife leaves her husband and is unfaithful. The husband wonders what to do and decides to lure her back. He pursues her to lead her out of the wilderness. He speaks to her heart.

The God of Israel is in pursuit of his people. He touches their hearts and they pursue him. The God of Israel pursues himself as his people pursue him. His passion becomes their passion. His question becomes their question. His quest becomes their quest. His prayer becomes their prayer. God is the question of "Man," *as* "Man" is the question of God. God is the question of "Man" *because* "Man" is the question of God. And so we read in Psalm 42:

> As a doe longs
>   for running streams,
> so longs my soul
>   for you, my God.
>
> My soul thirsts for God,
>   the God of life;
> when shall I go to see
>   the face of God? (Psalm 42:1-2)

This longing for God is often expressed in the form of a contention. The innocent Job cries out from his sadness. He curses the day of his birth:

> Why did I not die new-born,
>   not perish as I left the womb? (Job 3:11)

Job vacillates between trust and fear:

> Oh may my prayer find fulfilment,
>   may God grant me my hope!

28

But have I the strength to go on waiting?
What use is life to me, when doomed to certain
death?
Is mine the strength of stone,
or is my flesh bronze?
Can any power be found within myself,
has not all help deserted me? (Job 6:8,11-13)

Job cries out to his God. He feels alone and deserted. His cry is his question. It wracks his spirit and his body. He is his question.

The poet of the Psalms also cries out in anguish:

. . . For ever?
How much longer will you hide your face from me?
How much longer must I endure grief in my soul,
and sorrow in my heart by day and by night? . . .
(Psalm 13:1-2)

In Psalm 88, the lament becomes even stronger and more detailed:

Yahweh my God, I call for help all day,
I weep to you all night. (Psalm 88:1)

The psalmist is alone, forgotten, cast into the depths of darkness, repulsive to his friends. His God is absent from him. He is absent from his God.

Nor is Jesus excused from such anguish, from such cries. In the garden called Gethsemane, he prays: "My Father, . . . if it is possible, let this cup pass me by. . . ." (Matthew 26:39) And "In his anguish he prayed even more earnestly, and his sweat fell to the ground like great drops of blood." (Luke 22:44)

Jesus' question is spoken with his entire being. But another element enters, an element that is not lacking in Job or in the

Psalms. This is the deep trust in God expressed when Jesus says: "Nevertheless, let it be as you, not I, would have it." (Matthew 26:39)

The foundation of the questioning is a deeply felt and known trust. Yet, there is also uncertainty. There is the question.

This faith and openness is also manifest in Mary who asked: " . . . How can this come about, since I am a virgin?" (Luke 1:34) It is the faith of a Martha who protested: " . . . If you had been here, my brother would not have died, but I know that, even now, whatever you ask of God, he will grant you." (John 11:21-22)

Questioning and Faith

There is an Hasidic story which deftly illustrates this relationship between faith and questioning. It is called *The Fiftieth Gate:*

> Without telling his teacher anything of what he was doing, a disciple of Rabbi Barukh's had inquired into the nature of God, and in his thinking had penetrated further and further until he was tangled in doubts, and what had been certain up to this time, became uncertain. When Rabbi Barukh noticed that the young man no longer came to see him as usual, he went to the city where he lived, entered his room unexpectedly, and said to him: "I know what is hidden in your heart. You have passed through the fifty gates of reason. You begin with a question and think, and think up an answer — and the first gate opens, and to a new question! And again you plumb it, find the solution, fling open the second gate — and look into a new question. On and on like this, deeper and deeper, until you have forced open the fiftieth gate. There you stare at a question whose

30

answer no man has ever found, for if there were one who knew it, there would no longer be freedom of choice. But if you dare to probe any further, you plunge into the abyss." "So I should go back all the way, to the very beginning," cried the disciple. "If you turn, you will not be going back," said Rabbi Barukh. "You will be standing beyond the last gate; you will stand in faith."[10]

The disciple will not deny his questioning. He will simply stand in a different place. His question will not be answered. He will simply stand in faith, the faith not of a beginner but of a man who has crossed the river and now must continue his journey.

"Man" is the question of God — and this is why Matthew can say: " . . . your Father knows what you need before you ask him." (Matthew 6:8)

The questioner becomes the question. The pray-er becomes the prayer. "Ask, and it will be given to you; search, and you will find; knock, and the door will be opened to you. For the one who asks always receives; the one who searches always finds; the one who knocks will always have the door opened to him." (Matthew 7:7-8)

The searching is the finding, the knocking is the opening. This asking is founded on faith, as expressed in the Gospel According to John:

If you remain in me
and my words remain in you,
you may ask what you will
and you shall get it. (John 15:7)

Finally, a very profound question that many of us ask either consciously or unconsciously is uttered by Rabbi Levi Yitzhak. His question does not arise at a special moment or because of an unusual happening. His question is one that can be asked by any person, anytime, anywhere. What did Levi Yitzhak ask? He cried out to his God that he was not interested in the secret of the divine ways. He murmured:

> But show me one thing; show it to me more clearly and deeply; show me what this very moment, what is happening at this very moment, means to me, what it demands of me, what you, Lord of the World, are telling me by way of it.[11]

Prayer, then, is a question: God's question addressed to us and our questions addressed to God. Prayer is just as much the questions we pose to life and those by which life challenges us. These questions are transparent in our day-to-day wonderings and wanderings, expectations and longings, fears and tremblings, demands and periods of quiet. The questions arise out of the depth of life and also from its surface. They are grounded in a trust which does not deny or forego the questions, but now asks them from the heart.

Notes

1. Marilyn Harris, *Hatter Fox* (New York: Bantam, 1974), pp. 8-9.
2. Thomas Merton, *Contemplative Prayer* (New York: Herder and Herder, 1969), p. 26.
3. Elie Wiesel, *Night* (New York: Avon, 1969), pp. 13-14.
4. Thomas P. McDonnell, ed., *A Thomas Merton Reader* (New York: Harcourt, Brace and World, 1962), p. 373.
5. Elie Wiesel, *A Beggar in Jerusalem* (New York: Avon, 1971), pp. 15-16.
6. Ibid., p. 172.
7. Idries Shah, *The Pleasantries of the Incredible Mulla Nasrudin* (New York: Dutton, 1971), p. 87.

8. Elie Wiesel, *The Town Beyond the Wall* (New York: Avon, 1969), p. 187.

9. D. T. Suzuki, *The Field of Zen* (New York: Perennial Library, 1970), p. 15.

10. Martin Buber, *Tales of the Hasidim: The Early Masters* (New York: Schocken, 1947), p. 92.

11. Ibid., pp. 212-213.

3

Prayer as Wonder

Openness to Mystery

As a radical questioning at the root of life, a questioning that arises from the very situation of life, prayer involves a sense of wonder. Often, when we question, we say: "I wonder." As we saw earlier, questioning involves an openness to mystery in life. Wonder is a vibrant entry into that mystery.

Saint-Exupery's Little Prince is a wondering person. The Little Prince asks many questions, gentle questions, wondering questions. For example, as his friend the pilot describes an airplane to him, the Prince cries out, "What! You dropped from the sky?" His question contains an element of "unbelief," and an element of wonder.[1]

The Prince is also a lover of sunsets. One day, on a small planet, he sees the sunset forty-four times. He wonders. Yet, he is also sad: "One loves the sunset, when one is so sad," he muses.

Wonder is not only joyful. It can also be sad. The Prince also has great difficulty with adults who are always involved with "matters of consequence." Their wonder is restricted to what is important. The Prince does not deny the importance of those matters, he simply extends importance to simple things like mushrooms and roses and sheep and hats and elephants. His wonder is inclusive rather than exclusive. The Little Prince is open to the mystery, to what he sees and what he doesn't see. He is a wondering person.

The Little Prince embodies the experience of wonder in three ways. The first two ways are similar to each other; they both pertain directly to questioning.

First, there is a curiosity which has the flavor of active seeking.

Then there is a questioning which is more subtle than curiosity. It is expressed in the soft, gentle, reflective murmur: "I wonder." I call it a gentle questioning.

Finally, wonder is an exclamation which is expressive of marvel.

Experiencing the Present

While it may have some leanings toward the future, wonder is a very present experience.

It is experienced in that one moment when the ocean is striking in its vastness and greenness and movement and power and gentleness.

It is the marvel that a conversation has taken place, or that there can really be a relationship with this particular person.

It is the feeling that spring has finally come after a long winter.

It is contained in the exclamation: "I can be alive, I can breathe, I can see, I can feel the wind on my body."

It is the realization that there is laughter, creativity, rest, endings, beginnings, insight.

It is the feeling and realization that something has finally gone well.

It is the joy of openness to the world, to nature, to other human persons.

Wonder, in fact, can be experienced as a "mini-vacation" in the midst of labor and pain and striving. Wonder is the joy of questioning. It is the curious seeking that is so totally self-engaging that one is really unself-conscious, yet very involved in the relationship that is present at the moment. These experiences tell us something about prayer. They are integral to prayer. I would go so far as to say that they *are* prayer.

Such wonder or marvel is often expressed in Japanese haiku poetry. The haiku "captures" the wonder of a moment in which the author is fully present in that place at that moment. A person "sees" a flower, and both the person and the flower are transparent. This transparency is evident in the well-known haiku by Basho:

> When I look carefully
> I see the nazuna blooming
> By the hedge![2]

The "capture" is paradoxical; the haiku does not merely "hold" the moment but also frees it by noticing it in wonder.

Another good example is to be found in a poetic comment on one of my favorite haiku poems, "On Basho's Frog":

> Under the cloudy cliff, near the temple door,
> Between dusky spring plants on the pond,
> A frog jumps in the water, plop!
> Startled, the poet drops his brush.[3]

Wonder and Curiosity

But the power of wonder can be blocked. In the Gospel According to Luke, we read of an encounter between Jesus and his disciples. The disciples were arguing among themselves about which one was the greatest. What we see here is a group of men, each of whom felt he had the answer, a group of men who were very self-conscious. No one of them was curious about what the others felt or knew. They were arguing over position and status (Luke 9:46).

This kind of argument rules out curiosity. It is the argument from authority, in which a person argues from a superior position. Having heard, or used, this argument from authority many times, we all know that it usually cuts off the discussion very quickly. It weakens the spirit of curiosity and deadens wonder.

In the Gospel According to Matthew, Jesus is approached by his disciples with the question: "Who is the greatest in the kingdom of heaven?" Jesus responds by calling a little child to himself and saying: "I tell you solemnly, unless you change and become like little children you will never enter the kingdom of heaven. And so, the one who makes himself as little as this little child is the greatest in the kingdom of heaven." (Matthew 18:1-4)

In one way of understanding this elusive passage, Jesus is referring to the openness and curiosity of children. Children do not believe that they have all the answers. Children can wonder. They have not yet developed an authority complex as Jesus' disciples had.

Who is the greatest? The greatest is the one who can wonder, who can seek, and who can be curious.

Wonder and Longing

Wonder also involves a sense of longing. There is an element of future here, but it is not prominent. On the surface, longing may seem to be a "wanting-something-to-happen" which seems almost impossible. Longing, however, arises out of a mood which is very present, a present sense of limitation with a strong sense of something "more" which goes beyond the question of whether or not the "more" is possible. Longing is closely related to — but not the same as — "expectation."

During the past summer a friend provided me with some understanding of this kind of longing. The day was overcast; clouds hid the sun and a mist filtered its rays. It had been this way for a few weeks. There had been moments when sunlight would break between the clouds, but these moments were few and brief. My friend longed for the sun. A day could be more than it has been. But when? The question is a strong, gentle, wondering question.

Again, it would seem that expectation is very future-oriented. This future is not isolated, however, from the past nor from the present. The past is not all there is, nor is the present. Or, to put it better, to expect is to see into the present in its fullness. Maurice Friedman speaks of hope in this way, as the pregnancy of the present. There is more to the present than meets the eye. And when it does meet the eye, that present becomes *wonder-full*. It is here that visions — seeings — are born.

There is a passage in the Book of Isaiah and another in the Book of Revelation which give expression to the wonder of which I have spoken. The authors of these passages were not given to naïve, idealistic dreams of the future. Both authors had done a lot of living in situations which were very painful. They cry out from these situations and their cry is a cry of wonder and longing. In Isaiah we read:

> I shall rejoice over Jerusalem and exult in my people. No more will the sound of weeping or the sound of cries be heard in her; . . . To die at the age of a hundred will be dying young; not to live to be a hundred will be the sign of a curse. They will build houses and inhabit them, plant vineyards and eat their fruit. They will not build for others to live in, or plant so that others can eat. For my people shall live as long as trees, and my chosen ones wear out what their hands have made. They will not toil in vain or beget children to their own ruin, . . . Long before

they call I shall answer; before they stop speaking I
shall have heard. (Isaiah 65:19-24)

The author of the Book of Revelation almost repeats what is
wondered by Isaiah. While speaking of a New Jerusalem, of a
new heaven and a new earth, he writes:

> . . . Here God lives among men. He will make *his
> home among them; they shall be his people*, and he
> will be their God; his name is *God-with-them. He
> will wipe away all tears from their eyes;* there will be
> no more death, and no more mourning or sadness.
> The world of the past has gone. (Revelation 21:3-4)

Imagine — no one dies, no more tears, living as long as trees,
not begetting children to their own ruin! These are not visions of
a future Utopia; they are flights of imaginative wonder in which
is expressed a profound compassion. They are a few brief
moments when the pain has become eased.

Passages like these are not confined to people who lived
thousands of years ago. They are found even among our con-
temporaries. Even a man like Daniel Berrigan, who is deeply
aware of the inhumanity in our world and who spent months in
prison, could exclaim:

> I hope (imagine!) no one dies. No one dies. I mean
> the final glacial death — into hopelessness, into
> violence, into power that is empty of conscience,
> into dread and nausea and inaction and egoism and
> base fear.[4]

Imagine, just imagine, Berrigan can still wonder; and from that
wonder arises a vision, not of the future merely, but of the
present and its pregnancy.

Sadness and Joy

Hatter Fox is a fictional character who also can still wonder. In the previous chapter we met Teague Summer, the doctor who was haunted by Hatter, and we listened to some of his questions. In the eyes of most people, Hatter was a social deviant who should have been locked up and the key thrown away. Summer, however, stayed with her defiance and rejection of him and society. And, in time, she began to open up to him. What did Summer see? He saw a young woman who as a child had lived in many homes, a child who was abused by everyone, a young girl who at times supported herself by being a fraternity prostitute.

Hatter was bitter and angry and defiant. It would seem that she could not wonder. Yet, as Summer was to discover, deep in Hatter's soul, heavily guarded and protected, was a gentle vision of natural beauty. This vision broke through her protective walls on a quiet afternoon when she and Summer were in the hills near Albuquerque. Hatter's vision is a challenge to us, yet it also expresses her own hidden but still present ability to wonder. Speaking of Albuquerque, she says:

> I wish they would go away and let the fields have it back. Let the fields and the canyons and the mountains have it all back, the empty space beneath the sky. Clear all that away, send the people packing back to where they came from. Let the fields and sky and mountains fill the empty space until it isn't empty any longer.[5]

Not only is there wonder in this vision of a "virgin wilderness," there is also a deep sadness. Sadness and wonder are not inconsistent. Hatter expresses such sadness as she recognizes the impossibility of her vision, but her question also contains another sad wonder. She asks: "Summer, do you ever feel like nothing in the world is ever going to be the way it should be?"[6]

Weeping can express a variety of feelings and experiences. It can be painful, and it can be wondrous. Weeping can express suffering, the pain of "too much" or the tears of "not enough." Weeping can also give expression to people's discovery of a way to deal with their pain. Painful weeping may contain the tears of an empty vision, the feeling that there is no way out. Joyful weeping may contain the tears of a fulfilled vision, the feeling that there is a way open.

Isaiah and the author of the Book of Revelation speak of, and to, both these kinds of weeping. For those who weep painful tears, the biblical authors simply describe the pain, so that those who are suffering it know that someone affirms them in their pain without denying the pain or denying their helpless feeling. This response itself is a wonder. It can engender the sense that "someone knows my condition and does not belittle it."

For those who weep joyful tears, the biblical sages describe their condition and then give expression to their vision. And this too is wonderful!

While all this seems to be irrational and out of the ordinary, it arises out of the depths of the ordinary. It contains the unreasonable wonder expressed in the words of Jesus: " . . . the kingdom of God is close at hand." (Mark 1:15)

Caught Up in Wonder

There is a fascination here which, as Rudolf Otto points out, is an element of the experience of the holy. Fascination is the opposite of indifference. To be indifferent is to withhold oneself and one's attention. It is to view everyone and everything in the same manner. Indifference is passionlessness. To be fascinated, however, is to feel deeply and to be attentive and to relish the uniqueness of a person or place or thing or moment. To be fascinated is to be grasped, held, caught in fear and trembling, trust and confidence. It is to pray with Paul:

This, then, is what I pray, kneeling before the Father, from whom every family, whether spiritual or natural, takes its name:

Out of his infinite glory, may he give you the power through his Spirit for your hidden self to grow strong, so that Christ may live in your hearts through faith, and then, planted in love and built on love, you will with all the saints have strength to grasp the breadth and the length, the height and the depth; until, knowing the love of Christ, which is beyond all knowledge, you are filled with the utter fullness of God. (Ephesians 3:14-19)

Praying persons wonder; they are caught by the subject of their wonder in such a way that they are confident in the wonder and questioning, trustful in the searchings. Or, to put this a bit more mildly — they can keep going and yet cry out in the spirit of Paul that *"no eye has seen and no ear has heard, things beyond the mind of man, all that God has prepared for those who love him."* (1 Corinthians 2:9)

These brief moments of wonder can give courage and strength to act or to be quiet. It is like the man who found a treasure hidden in a field and for sheer joy went and sold all he had to buy that field. The point here is not that he sold all he had to buy the field. The point is that he was caught up in his wonder, that he went beyond himself and could extend himself in action.[7]

Wonder can also produce the energy by which people will dedicate their lives to certain pursuits. Such was the experience of Pierre Teilhard de Chardin. Stories are told of how he wept when he saw a human hair consumed by the flames in the hearth of his childhood home; or of how he roamed through the fields and roads and woods, looking for anything durable such as rocks or bits of crystal; and finally, how, at the age of six, he exclaimed with wonder and admiration when he came upon a piece of iron from an old plough: "My iron — my divine iron."[8]

This wonder at the things of the earth never left Teilhard. He was caught by it and freed by it. His wonder invigorated his lifelong search for the innerness of matter. In *The Divine Milieu,* after speaking of the burden of matter, he was able to say that:

> Matter is physical exuberance, ennobling contact, virile effort and the joy of growth. It attracts, renews, unites and flowers. By matter we are nourished, lifted up, linked to everything else, invaded by life. To be deprived of it is intolerable. . . . Who will give us an immortal body?[9]

It is in the light and strength and energy of such a wonder that Teilhard lived his life with sensitivity and courage.

Dance of Wonder

The joy of wonder is also magnificently expressed in the dancing of the Hasid. It is a moment of joy that enters briefly into the hardness of daily life. It is told of the dancing of one rabbi:

> His foot was as light as that of a four-year-old child. And among all who saw his holy dancing, there was not one in whom the holy turning was not accomplished, for in the hearts of all who saw he worked both weeping and rapture in one.[10]

Can we still dance like this today? The rabbi was burdened with the sorrows and longings of his people. He wept. Yet he danced. And the weeping and the rapture became one. These men lived in such a way that the suffering of their people was transformed for a few moments. Their downcast souls were recreated. They stood out from themselves for a few hours. One Hasidic master spoke of the recreation in the following words:

> The creation of heaven and of earth is the unfolding of something out of nothing, the descent of the higher into the lower. But the holy men who detach themselves from being and ever cleave to God see and comprehend him in truth, as if there was now the nothing as before creation. They turn the something back into nothing. And this is the more wonderful: to raise up what is beneath. As it is written: "The last wonder is greater than the first."[11]

Such dancing does exist today. It goes on not only in an Hasidic synagogue, where I experienced it a few years ago with Rabbi Shlomo Carlbach, but also in the streets of Moscow. In 1965 and 1966 Elie Wiesel visited Moscow. He was drawn by the silent cry of the Jews of that land. It was the evening of the feast of Simchat Torah, the celebration of the completion of the reading of the Torah. Jews — young and old, poor and rich, educated and uneducated, believers and unbelievers, those who are Jews only in name and birth and those who are committed Jews — all these Jews, thousands of them (thirty or forty thousand by some counts), gathered outside the Central Synagogue. Many of these people were suffering from some kind of persecution. Their lives were steeped in fear. Yet, they gathered publicly at the synagogue, "where they remained until almost dawn singing and dancing in Hasidic abandon."[12] For a few hours they were raised up and recreated. Their political situation did not change. But they were able to enter into it again with a bit more energy and courage. And by their wonder they continue to challenge our wonder.

Persons caught in despair have little energy left for action. They feel that nothing really matters, that nothing will really change. And yet, they realize that they have no choice but to continue on. To dance for a few moments, to long for a few moments, to wonder for a few moments — this does not change their condition in life. It merely lifts them. They are quickened. "There are those who suffer very greatly and cannot tell what is in their hearts, and they go their ways full of suffering. But, if they meet someone whose face is bright with laughter, he can quicken them with his gladness. And it is no small thing to quicken a human being!"[13]

Prayer of Wonder

Finally, I would like to introduce you to a wonder-ful elderly lady. She is a fictional person. This lady, full of wonder, is a character in a novel and a film. Her name is Countess Mathilda Chardin, but she is commonly known as Maude. Maude is a survivor of a Nazi concentration camp. Her interests range from funerals to a field of daisies, from births to motorcycles. Even though she is near her eightieth birthday, Maude is an explorer and always open to a new experience. Her wonder extends to anything and everything. She grows excited at a freshly baked cake as well as at munching on a raw carrot. Everything and everyone is precious for Maude, so precious that she is un-possessive; she can throw a gift in the lake and exclaim: "Now I'll always know where it is."[14] On one occasion Maude attempts to share her spirit with a young man named Harold. That spirit is summed up in her words to him when he finds her crying. She says:

> Yes. I cry. I cry for you. I cry for this [an old visa]. I cry at beauty — a sunset or a seagull. I cry when a man tortures his brother . . . when he repents and begs forgiveness . . . when forgiveness is refused . . . and when it is granted. One laughs. One cries. Two uniquely human traits. And the main thing in life, my dear Harold, is not to be afraid to be human.[15]

45

Maude is filled with wonder, a wonder that is at the source of her smile as well as of her tears. She is a person whom we know we cannot imitate. She is inimitable. Yet, she allows us to be free to smile and laugh and cry and, in all this, to be wonderers. She can quicken another human person. "And it is no small thing to quicken a human being."

This is the prayer of wonder — for some to be quickened and for others to quicken. This is the marvel, the longing, the expectation, the curiosity, the gentle questioning. It is the coming alive for a few moments. And this itself is a marvel, a wonder.

Notes

1. Antoine de Saint-Exupery, *The Little Prince* (New York: Harcourt, Brace and World, 1943), p. 13.
2. Quoted in D. T. Suzuki, E. Fromm, R. DeMartino, *Zen Buddhism and Psychoanalysis* (New York: Grove, 1963), p. 1.
3. Lucien Stryk, Takoshi Ikemoto, ed. & trans., *Zen: Poems, Prayers, Sermons, Anecdotes, Interviews* (New York: Anchor, 1963), p. 17.
4. Daniel Berrigan as quoted by Robert Heyer, ed., *Discovery in Word* (New York: Paulist, 1968), p. 124.
5. Marilyn Harris, *Hatter Fox* (New York: Bantam, 1974), p. 219.
6. Ibid., p. 219.
7. Cf. Matthew 13:44-46. It is interesting to note how the wonder can be taken from discovery by the law. A friend who is a law student mentioned to me that this particular parable of the treasure would be senseless in England because the man who found the treasure and spent his fortune would have wasted his worldly lot. Why? Treasure trove, by law, belongs to the crown, not to its finder or to the owner of the land where it is found. Hence, the law

would dissipate the joy and wonder of discovery, unless, of course, the finder were the king or queen.

8. Cf. Cecile Bolling v. Goetz, "Christian mystic, scientist, priest," *The National Catholic Reporter* (February 17, 1965), p. 9.
9. Pierre Teilhard de Chardin, *The Divine Milieu* (New York: Harper and Row, 1960), p. 82.
10. Martin Buber, *The Legend of the Baal-Shem* (New York: Schocken, 1969), p. 21.
11. Ibid., p. 23.
12. Elie Wiesel, *Legends of Our Time* (New York: Avon, 1970), p. 184.
13. Martin Buber, *Ten Rungs: Hasidic Sayings* (New York: Schocken, 1962), pp. 44-45.
14. Colin Higgins, *Harold and Maude* (New York: Avon, 1975), p. 122.
15. Ibid., p. 126.

4

Prayer as Silence

Silence Beyond Words

Wonder can often give rise to silence, the wonderful gaze, the speechless tongue, the receptive heart-mind. To believe that life is mystery is to believe that beyond and in words there is silence. Mystery gives rise to wonder, which precipitates silence, which itself is the mystery.

Moshe, the teacher of Elie Wiesel, said that our questions would be answered by God but that we would not be able to understand the answer. To question is to take the risk of not understanding an answer if one comes. A further risk, however, is that of receiving no answer at all. No matter which predominates, there is silence.

Of the many kinds of silence there are two of which I will speak: an uneasy silence and a creative silence. Silence surrounds us. It can give rise to fear as in the tears of a young child left alone in a dark room at night.

Or, it can caress you as the silence of the night while walking on a beach or through a forest.

Or, it can create you as when the poet or painter rises to pen the words that have been yearning to be said or to paint that picture which has teased the imagination.

Silence can be a bridge to others, or it can divide a person from self and from others. It can be filled with joy, and it can be filled with hurt and bitterness. Silence can be sterile, or it can be creative. The second is what we seek, but how often we encounter the first!

I will speak first of the uneasy silence, which may at times have the seeds of creative silence within it.

Uneasy Silence

At the beginning of a semester, when many of my students are not yet totally familiar with my teaching style, some of these students experience an uneasy, anxious silence in class. Often after I ask a question of the class, a silence will take over the room. It is a time to think. The seconds pass slowly for some students. The silence becomes loud and anxious for them. For others, it is a quiet time for reflection. The uneasiness of the silence for some students is symptomatic of a difficulty some persons have with silence at any time. Something must be going on for these people at all times. They cannot stand the silence.

Another uneasy silence is heavy. A group of people sit together conversing quietly. Suddenly, someone enters the room and announces that he has a message. The room becomes quiet with expectation. The man then communicates some bad news. His words are punctuated by silence. When he is finished, silence again takes over. The initial expectant silence has been transformed into an uneasy, sad silence.

Or, there is the silence of Hatter Fox who, while confined to her cell, refuses to speak with anyone. There is no one who has ever listened to her. She feels that no one will even hear her. Why, then, should she speak? Her silence is a challenge. It defies. And those who can hear this defiant silence also become uneasy.

There is also an oppressive silence — the silence that was experienced by people being escorted by a Nazi SS officer to a barracks in a concentration camp where they were left standing, waiting. This is the silence of people being treated unjustly.

And then there is a stoney silence, the silence of a hardened heart, the silence of a person expecting not to be heard and, hence, unable to risk a word.

In the Book of Ecclesiastes, Qoheleth proclaims: " . . . Vanity of vanities. All is vanity! For all his toil, his toil under the sun, what does man gain by it?" (Ecclesiastes 1:2-3) A person comes face-to-face with his or her own finiteness or impermanence, with the perishableness of all that is done. There is nothing that has substance. All is empty. All is void. The silence that may engulf us when we come face-to-face with this condition may be creative, but it is more often uneasy. There is nothing to gain. All things pass. What is the use in even getting up in the morning? Nothing will grow in this desert where I am, in this desert who I am. Nothing can speak to my situation. The situation itself does not speak. This is a silence which is anxious, which leaves us helpless. Something of what I am trying to say is expressed in the following:

> Hard turf silently softens under
> the gaze of a warm
> sun.
> a debilitating lethargy seeps slowly
> into the bones — or out —
> so slowly and almost
> imperceptibly.
> Both wanted and unwanted it is
> allowed to filter through
> the body to the
> mind.
> There is nowhere to turn — it
> can't be stopped —
> Familiar faces, longing eyes, encouraging,

voice, unspoken words, spanning hundreds
of miles — maybe a few feet,
the sound of a smooth guitar,
    a light voice,
        passion;
a paperback which once spoke so
    eloquently — why not
        now?
a God who is silent in the emptiness
    of the phony —
nothing can satisfy,
    nothing contain the flow,
    no thing really matters —
what was alive in the morning is a
    forgotten dream as the
        body sags under the burden
            of a bloodless heart.
everyone and no one is near,
    as the unidentified self
        reaches out and can't
say a word — for there is no word —
    just blankness
that unsettles the stomach
    in the face of a day
        which has no promise,
a now which is dead and
    a past which is a
        dream.
you bite your finger or tongue;
but that is disappointing — no
    thing, no one can
        fill the gap,
            so why . . .
(even that can be disconcerting)
            . . . bother?

forget in the passage of a deep sleep?
it will return — it won't let go —
a few days or weeks, maybe — but
then . . .

Dark Silence

These have been a few examples of experiences that might give birth to an uneasy silence. But there is another uneasy silence which is more ambivalent. This silence is given expression by Isaiah when he says:

The people that walked in darkness
has seen a great light;
on those who live in a land of deep shadow
a light has shone. (Isaiah 9:1)

The silence is that of darkness, I might even say the dark night of the soul — a time of purgation, of purification. The storm is raging. A direction is seen. But it is not yet taken. Is there the energy to go where I see I can go? Elie Wiesel suggests: "It is in the silence after the storm that God reveals himself to man. God is silence."[1]

In this silence after the storm we expect to be on the shore, but there is no land on the horizon. It is then that we can cry out with Isaiah:

Yahweh, can you go unmoved by all of this,
oppressing us beyond measure by your silence?
(Isaiah 64:11-12)

A response may return to us, again through Isaiah:

From the beginning I have been silent,
I have kept quiet, held myself in check.

I groan like a woman in labour,
I suffocate, I stifle. (Isaiah 42:14)

This is the God who spoke, and light was shed on the world.
This is the God who creates, yet finds so many obstacles in the
way of "his" creative power. "He" is long overdue. In "his"
labor "he" is suffocating, stifled. Maybe this is what Dietrich
Bonhoeffer meant when he wrote: "Man is challenged to
participate in the sufferings of God at the hands of a godless
world."[2]

The godless person — who may or may not believe in God —
is the one who refuses to allow silence to speak creatively. To
participate in the sufferings of God may be to search continuously for new ways to create in the midst of a suffocating,
stifling cloud. It is being able to continue on, to rise out of bed in
the morning and not know why or how it is done.

Thomas Merton describes in detail the silence of which I am
speaking, though he uses very different language. Speaking of
prayer in solitude in his book *Contemplative Prayer,* he points
out that the dimensions of this type of prayer "are those of
man's ordinary anguish, his self-searching, his moments of
nausea at his own vanity, falsity, and capacity for betrayal."[3]
These are some of the elements of the ambiguity of which I
spoke above: an exhilarating uneasiness and an agonizing creativity.

Creative Silence

In order to be creative, the silence of prayer demands an
intense listening by the one praying, a listening not only to his or
her own heart but also to the heart of the world. Merton
develops this point in regard to the prayer of the monk, though
he does not exclude the layperson who is also called to be a
person of prayer. Merton writes:

This is an age that, by its nature as time of crisis, of revolution, of struggle, calls for the special searching and questioning which are the work of the monk in his meditation and prayer. For the monk searches not only his heart: he plunges deep into the heart of that world of which he remains a part although he seems to have "left" it. In reality the monk abandons the world only in order to listen more intently to the deepest and most neglected voices that proceed from its inner depth.

In the silence which is darkness and exile and even despair, the worst is faced. In the silence there can be listening. And out of that listening, a hearing. And from the hearing. . . .

There are other times, however, when silence means rest and quiet. The silent meditative prayer is not so much a way to the finding of God (which we still attempt) but, rather, a way of resting in the God who is near, whose presence is felt among us. This presence was described in the previous chapter on prayer as wonder. Wonder is a standing silent in the presence of the One who is to come and who is with us. This silence is not the silence of noiselessness, nor is it the silence of boredom. It is, rather, the silence of "isness" which is "becoming."

Many people object to this kind of silence. "It is a waste of time," they might say, or, "What use does it have?" We are so used to having well-defined goals and putting our time to good use that we cannot forget about time. We get caught in time. But the silence of which I am now speaking is utterly useless. It does not have a goal. Hence, it cannot be exploited.

We attempt to gain status or success, power or pleasure, meaning or self-fulfillment. No one of these is the ultimate answer. At each point we return to silence. Silence has nothing to gain nor to lose. We contemporary people do. We cannot stand being useless for very long. We must have a goal or purpose. But that very purpose or goal can give rise to anxiety and frustration. And so often it can also give rise to exploitation: stepping on another person to reach that goal we set for ourselves. But silence is useless. In this it is pure. It exists for nothing at all, yet by that very fact encompasses all. It is the nothing created out of something.

In the same way, prayer is useless. It serves no practical purpose, not even to relax the one praying. For once a person tries to relax, the very trying becomes an obstacle to relaxing. But once a person lets go, then the relaxation enters and the silence becomes pure. The silence enters with its creative power.

Finally, this silence does not have to happen only in a meditation hall or a chapel or even in one's room. It can happen there. But it can also happen when one is speaking or working or walking. For, in work which is really work and in speech which is really speech — that is, related work and related speech — silence is always present. In his novel *Dawn,* Wiesel has one of his characters saying: "For half an hour, an hour, we walked in complete silence. At first I found the silence embarrassing, then to my surprise I began to enjoy it. The silence of two people is deeper than the silence of one. Involuntarily, I began to talk."[5]

Silence is the context of the word and the deed. More than being their context, it is of their essence and substance. It is then a silence which thunders greatly!

Forms of Creative Silence

There are many other forms of creative silence. One is the thoughtful silence. A question is asked. The person questioned is not threatened but remains quiet for a few moments, gathering thoughts and organizing them. Then out of this reflective, thoughtful silence, a response is made.

Silence may also be healing. Imagine a day filled with constant demands, with barely time to breathe. There is a longing for at least a few moments of quiet, of silence, of time to gather one's resources and strength. One Hasidic master would go so far as to say that unless a person has one hour a day to himself or herself, that person will not be human. Silence is not only the substance of the word and the deed. Silence is of the essence of being human.

I will conclude this chapter with three Hasidic anecdotes. I will comment on the first and then allow the next two to speak for themselves.

Rabbi Mendel once commented on the verse in the Scriptures: "For God hath heard the voice of the lad." He explained it in this way: "Nothing in the preceding verses indicates that Ishmael cried out. No, it was a soundless cry, and God heard it."[6] What is a soundless cry? It is a silent cry. It is a cry from the heart, a cry that cannot or does not become a spoken word. Such a cry might express despair or hopelessness. But it also might be a person's only resistance to an uncontrollably painful existence. Nothing *said* would seem to be of help. Since such a cry comes from the heart, from a person's depth, it might be said that it is heard by God, the God who is the heart of our heart. But it might also be said that such a cry is heard by God, since it is uttered by God in the heart of the person crying. It is heard by the God who is in sympathy with the one crying.

Rabbi Mendel's *hasidim* once sat at his table in silence. The silence was so profound that one could hear a fly on the wall. After grace, the rabbi of Biala said to his neighbor: "What a table we had today! I was probed so deeply that I thought my veins would burst, but I managed to hold out and answer every question I was asked."[7]

When Mendel was in Kotzk, the rabbi of that town asked him: "Where did you learn the art of silence?" He was on the verge of answering the question, but then he changed his mind and practiced his art.[8]

56

Notes

1. Elie Wiesel, *The Gates of the Forest* (New York: Avon, 1967), p. 71.
2. Dietrich Bonhoeffer, *Letters and Papers from Prison* (New York: Macmillan, 1953), p. 222.
3. Thomas Merton, *Contemplative Prayer* (New York: Herder and Herder, 1969), p. 25.
4. Ibid.
5. Elie Wiesel, *Dawn* (New York: Avon, 1970), p. 67.
6. Martin Buber, *Tales of the Hasidim: The Later Masters* (New York: Schocken, 1948), p. 301.
7. Ibid.
8. Ibid.

5

Prayer as Concentration

Heart of the World

Raimundo Panikkar says that the essence of Hindu prayer could be summed up in one word — concentration. Often, when Oriental prayer is discussed, it is understood as a form of navel-gazing or a looking at one's nose or as a form of sophisticated introspection. Panikkar points out that this is precisely what it is not. He suggests that concentration is the finding of a center, the gathering around a point. It is the finding of the center of a sphere which is the whole of reality.

In Christian terms, this might be described as the reconciliation of all things in Christ. It also may be spoken of in terms of recollection (a gathering together again) or in terms of meditation (finding a center, a midst, a middle).

It is very important that we understand that *the center to be found is not our psychological ego.* Prayer as concentration is not a sophisticated form of egoism. It does not consist in becoming aware of my self, my ego, my private self. It is, rather, an awareness of living in a network of relations.

This last remark needs some clarification. We Westerners usually view the world and other people as separate from ourselves. We are quite aware of individuality and uniqueness. What I wish to suggest here (and it will be developed more extensively in the next chapter) is that reality is more than this; that, at its root, reality is a network of relations. While each human person is unique, he or she is also related to all other persons and to the world. The primary fact is that of relation. "In the beginning is the relation," declares Martin Buber.[1] Thus, self is not defined in terms of a separate ego or as isolated from all else. Rather, self is understood in relation.

Meditation may begin with a looking into our own heart, but it does not end there. For if we concentrate while looking at our own heart, we can discover that it is the heart of the world. In other words, we discover the network of relations.

Presence

One way of speaking of concentration is in terms of presence. If we think of ourselves simply as individuals, we tend to see our interrelationships in terms of juxtaposition; we see ourselves as side by side, but not interpenetrating. But for persons to be present to one another, and for the world to be present to them and them to the world, there must exist an intrinsic relationship. We do not simply stand side by side; there is an interpenetration of our very beings. The primary fact of existence is not "me" but "I in relation."

To concentrate is to become this primary fact, to become present in the already existing fact of the relationship — that is, to realize our radical interconnection with others and the world.

In the biblical account of the meeting between Moses and his God at the burning bush, we hear Yahweh speaking of himself as "I am who am." This statement is quite individualistic. Another translation of this statement is "I will be for you as who I am shall I be for you." This second translation contains the first one, but extends it and gives expression to a fundamental interrelationship between God and his people. God is for his people. He is related to them and hence present for them. This relationship is also expressed in the covenant. "I will be your God and you shall be my people." God and his people are present to each other. The center is designated. It is both God and his people.

Prayer as concentration has certain characteristics that point to the meaning of presence. Concentration and presence are often viewed as states of inertia or unawareness. The opposite is true: concentration is a gathering of energies that heightens awareness. It is the condition pointed to by Paul when he says:

Wake up from your sleep,
rise from the dead. . . . (Ephesians 5:14)

The awareness of which I speak here is not an overawareness, that is, an awareness centered on one's ego. It is an awareness of what I am doing, but not in such a way that the awareness gets in the way of the action. Such an awareness is itself a being present.

Sense of Proportion

The presence of which I am speaking can also be discussed in terms of a sense of proportion. This sense of proportion is exhibited by God in the story of Jonah. Most of us remember that Jonah was swallowed by a whale. But very few recall the conclusion. Jonah had been sent to the city of Nineveh to call the people there to repentance. A time limit was set when this great city would be destroyed. But the people repented and the disaster was averted. Jonah was very upset by this; he wanted God to destroy the city as promised. So now, Jonah left the city and sought shade from the burning sun. God saw to it that a castor-oil plant should grow up over Jonah to give him shade. Jonah was delighted with the plant. The next day, God arranged that a worm should attack the plant, which it did, and the plant withered. Jonah was upset, even to the point of death. Yahweh said to him: "You are only upset about a castor-oil plant which cost you no labor. . . . Am I not to feel sorry for Nineveh?"

Jonah had lost all sense of proportion. He had become overly upset about a plant. God had been upset with the people of Nineveh, but when they repented he did not go ahead with his plans to destroy the city. God was not overly upset; he had retained a sense of proportion.

A sense of proportion is very much like the middle way of the Buddha. The phrase *middle way* is often interpreted as the avoidance of extremes in living, the finding of a balance. But if a person tries to find a balance, as difficult as this is, that person will always end up with some imbalance or with total inactivity. The middle way, however, is quite different. It is a relationship to life that life does not present itself as a choice between extremes. A person who is concentrated, who is present, can act with a sense of proportion without getting overly upset. For example, if I am not simply carried away by my emotion of rage or passivity, but choose the way I want to be, then I am concentrated, then I am involved, then I am "in the middle."

A sense of proportion might be misunderstood to be a balance. Not getting overly upset might also be seen as having the same attitude — calm — in every situation. But this is not what I mean by a sense of proportion. It is not a balance. Rather, it is a way of responding to what is demanded by the situation.

There is no one way to respond which might be called proportionate. Rather, the proportion is discovered in each unique situation. The response of a person in different situations may exhibit different degrees of "upsetness," more or less in accord with the demands. Thus, "not to get overly upset" does not mean the same attitude for all situations. It means "not getting overly upset" in this particular situation. Thus, I can be very upset — but not overly upset — in respect to one or another situation. The point is not so much the degree of

61

upsetness but, rather, a presence in the situation and a response to what the situation calls for.

Time

Another aspect of prayer as concentration involving presence is a sense of proportion in regard to time and space. Often, the past or the future might take over our lives. We might try to live in the past, or we might try to live only for the future. In both cases, the present is ignored. A sense of proportion about time overemphasizes neither the past nor the future; it allows them to tell us what they have to say in the present.

To be present is to live in the present. To live in the present is not a denial of the past and future but the integration of them. Living in the present, the full-time present, affirms the past as leading to itself and the future as leading from itself. But such full-time living is not only linear: past, then present, then future. The present is filled with both the past and the future, both of which make the present to be what it is.

It is generally clear to us how the past can be carried into the present. For example, memory involves the making present of the past. Also, from another angle, my past is part of what I am today.

However, it is often not as clear how the future impinges on the present. One might think: "The future has not happened yet. How can it be present?" Yet, we often do project ourselves into the future by plans made or goals or expectations. These projections enter into the present and affect our way of being present. Even if the ends have been unrealized, they have entered our present and shaped it to some extent. In other words, the future is projected into the present. Hence, full-time present is a present that is constituted by past and future not merely in a linear fashion but in a simultaneous fashion. Thus, one can live in the past and for the future simultaneously. To do this is to live in the present. A sense of proportion about time allows the past to be what it is in the present, allows the future to be what it is in the present, and allows the two to enter into a dialogue in the meeting of what is happening.

Space

A sense of proportion with respect to space can be seen in terms of place. There are many times when we might wish to be somewhere other than where we are at the moment. And there might be a good reason for this longing. Often, nothing can really be done to alter the circumstances. We can become overly upset, and the situation can become worse. A sense of proportion here would be neither to get out nor to give in. A sense of proportion, however, is not a sense of endurance. An Hasidic master once commented that the real exile of Israel in Egypt was that they began to endure it.

To be present is to be where we are when we are there, to do what we are doing when we are doing it. Soon after the death of Rabbi Moshe, Rabbi Mendel of Kotzk asked one of his disciples: "What was most important to your teacher?" The disciple replied: "Whatever he happened to be doing at the moment." To be present where you are, to do what you are doing, is to be related to it and to allow it to be related to you. This is not simply doing one thing at the time or place. It might mean being present to many things that are demanded at the moment. Often, concentration is incorrectly interpreted as doing one thing at a time. This interpretation, it seems to me, leaves too many people out — for example, parents or teachers who are called upon to respond to many calls at the same time. Concentration also means to be responsive to many simultaneous demands, deciding which one to respond to initially. It means establishing a hierarchy of values that sorts out whether each demand is to be met or only one or even none — depending on the demands and the resources one has for meeting those demands.

To be present in terms of doing what one is doing is to find the relationship which exists at the moment and to express that relationship in the action. The moment here is a full-time moment which contains the past, the present, and the future.

Compassion

Concentration, presence, and a sense of life as a network of relations. Flowing directly from these ways of being is a deep compassion for all living creatures.

Compassion is an essential element of prayer, no matter what religious tradition is being expounded. In the Jewish Scriptures, for example, one way compassion is given expression is in terms of love of the stranger:

> It is he who sees justice done for the orphan and the widow, who loves the stranger and gives him food and clothing. Love the stranger then, for you were strangers in the land of Egypt. (Deuteronomy 10:18-19)

Such love is not a patronizing love, but a love which derives from a communion between the people involved. It arises out of a sense of relation in the network of relations.

This spirit of compassion is also given expression in the famous Hindu classic, the *Bhagavad Gita*. While speaking of the true yogi who sees God in all things and all things in God and who is in union with that God, the author adds:

> Who burns with the bliss
> And suffers the sorrow
> Of every creature
> Within his own heart,
> Making his own
> Each bliss and each sorrow

Him I hold the highest
Of all the yogis.[2]

The true yogi is not simply isolated from others in meditative splendor. Rather, the true yogi can feel and think and be identified with any other person in joy or in sorrow, in pain or in bliss. The true yogi realizes more than the fact that he or she is related to other persons as members of the same species; the yogi also realizes that each of us is so immersed in a network of intrinsic relations with everyone else that each joy and sorrow is his or her own.

The same is true of the committed disciple of Jesus. Compassionate identification is at the heart of Jesus' eschatological discourse: " . . . I tell you solemnly, in so far as you did this to one of the least of these brothers of mine, you did it to me." (Matthew 25:40)

Compassionate identification is also embedded in the spirit of Hasidism. The Baal-Shem once exclaimed: "To pull another out of the mud, man must step into the mud himself."[3] Such a spirit is further expressed in this story that I will paraphrase from the tradition of Rabbi Nahman of Bratzlav:

In a far country, there lived a prince who lost his mind and thought that he was a dog. All day, he walked on all fours and would accept only scraps to eat. His father, the king, was desperate and sent for anyone — from medical specialists to miracle workers — to cure his son. All of them failed. Then an unknown sage came and said he thought he could cure the prince. The king allowed him to try. Immediately, the sage removed his clothes and joined the prince on the floor, barking and playing. Initially, the prince was upset and apprehensive. But gradually he accepted the sage-dog and the two became fast friends. Then the sage put on a shirt. The prince was unbelieving: "Why should a dog wear a shirt?" The sage responded: "We all know that a dog is a dog no matter what is being worn." The same conversation took place when the sage began to eat

65

like a human being, and then to act just like a human being. The prince followed suit and was convinced; he resumed his life as a prince.[4]

Prayer

To pray is to concentrate, which is to be present. To be present is to enter upon a work or a conversation or leisure without any obstacles. It is to meet the other as other and yet to be related to that person. It is to be able to make present as many of one's resources as are available at this time and place, no matter how great or small these resources may be. Even if there are no resources, this also can be made available. For example, if you are asked to do something or to listen to someone and you know that you cannot respond, you can communicate this fact to the person who is asking.

Prayer as concentration involves the focusing of one's self, the gathering together of energy, the being whole or integral which is holiness. Thus, it is not as important to say prayers as it is to *be* the prayer, to be whole, to be holy. The wholeness of which I speak is not an ideal unity but, rather, a wholeness of response in the present, a wholeness of response in proportion to one's resources in the present.

Prayer as concentration is not an escape from the world nor is it a substitute for action. One can act when action is called for and be still when quiet is demanded. This is the ever-active, ever-quiet spirit spoken of by Augustine of Hippo.

Prayer as concentration is not only a listening to the event or to the person; it is a realization of the communion with the world and other people that is the basic condition of each of us. Prayer as concentration means having one's roots dug into the heart of the world, into the Silence, which extends into our own hearts. This kind of prayer has no limits. It cannot be defined. Its only limits are those of authentic human existence itself. And that limit is Mystery.

Notes

1. Martin Buber, *I and Thou*, trans. W. Kaufmann (New York: Scribner, 1970), p. 69.
2. Swami Prabhavananda and Christopher Isherwood, trans., *Bhagavad Gita*, (New York: Mentor, 1944), p. 67.
3. Elie Wiesel, *Souls on Fire* (New York: Random House, 1972), p. 20.
4. Ibid., pp. 170-171.

6

Prayer as Relatedness

Prayer — A Network of Relations

Herman Melville wrote somewhere that "our lives are connected by a thousand threads." In the previous chapter, I referred to prayer as concentration in the context of reality as a network of relations. To concentrate is to gather our energies, to find a center that is not so much our individual ego as a center in a network of relations.

In the earlier chapters on prayer as questioning, wonder, and silence, the working assumption was the same — that reality is a network of relations. To question is to ask about that network, to seek out the connections and spaces in it. To wonder involves a curiosity about the network, a marveling and a fascination with it. To be silent is condition in which the connections or spaces may be either difficult to discern or — on the contrary — quietly realized and forged or felt to be ambiguous. Each of these experiences was seen to be prayer. Insofar as they are rooted in relatedness, then, the experience of relatedness is prayer.

It is the purpose of this chapter[1] to present a broad, panoramic view of reality — its structure and its dynamics — as a network of relations. The structure of the network, I would suggest, is the basic context of prayer. The dynamics of the network are the activities of prayer. Prayer is both the realization and actualization of the network, the being and doing of the network.

The network of relations in which we are involved is quite complex. It may be broadly described, using a word coined by Raimundo Panikkar, as "cosmotheandric."[2] This word attempts to join together three dimensions of reality that are often perceived today as separate: the world (*cosmo-*), the divine (*the-*), and the human (*andric*).

Relatedness happens within each of these three dimensions of reality as well as among them. Thus, in the cosmic dimension, relatedness involves nature. In the human dimension, relatedness involves the self and its relation with other selves. In the divine dimension, relatedness involves God's inner life. However, relatedness does not stop within the three dimensions; it is fundamental to the interplay of the three dimensions. The world, the human, and the divine dimensions of reality are inextricably related with each other. Thus, relatedness *within* self, nature, and God — as well as *among* self, nature, and God — is the realization of a cosmotheandric network of relations.

The life of each human person is a life in which some of these relations are recognized, some others recognized and realized, still others neither recognized nor realized, while others are strained. Life, in fact, can be seen as the continuous recognition and realization of the complex network of relations in which we live and move and are. It is my contention that the living of this life is to pray.

Relatedness is often understood to be a condition in which disunity and disharmony are replaced by unity or harmony. The unity of the cosmotheandric network, however, is a unity that involves diversity as necessary for itself. The network cannot be reduced to a basic unity nor to a mere juxtaposition of its major elements. Rather, this network is a unity in diversity and a diversity in unity.

Relatedness with Self

One essential "object" (or should I say "subject"?) of relatedness is the "self." During a typical day I might experience not myself but rather myselves, or the many different selves who I am. These many selves may be seen as "roles" that I would choose to play or into which I have flowed. Thus, I might experience myself as a teacher or a friend or a priest or a therapist or a student or an antagonist. Furthermore, in each of these "roles" I might experience myself in many different ways. I am not exactly the same self for each of my friends or for each of my students, and so on.

It might seem that, with so many roles and so many ways of being in each role, I would become confused. But this is not the case. Nor is it the case for very many people. Even though each of us is manifest in many different ways, we do not feel fragmented because of that. We rarely suffer the deep pain of one of my former students, who confided to me that she could not be with more than one friend at the same time. She felt very comfortable with each friend when they were alone together. But when she was in the presence of two or more of her friends, she did not know who to be. Her question was: What person should I be when I am with this person or with that person? This young woman felt the deep pain of fragmentation. Her many selves were separate. Most of us are, more or less, all of a piece, though each of us will suffer some form of fragmentation at some time or in some relationship. We human persons experience ourselves as a self and as selves. We are all of a piece — one self and many selves.

Congruence

Being all of a piece is the dynamic condition that psychologist Carl Rogers describes as being congruent. Most of us rarely use the word *congruent* in relation to ourselves. This word usually conjures up memories of high-school geometry, where we encountered congruent triangles or rectangles. One triangle is congruent to another if they fit exactly together. This geometric meaning is close to what Carl Rogers means by the term. Rogers suggests that he experiences congruence in himself when what he is experiencing is present also in his awareness and in his communication. His experience and awareness and communication fit together. They are all of a piece. The diverse elements of experience, awareness, and communication are a unity. It is during moments when this is so that Rogers feels himself to be congruent or "real."

I would also suggest that persons who experience themselves both as one self and as many selves can be congruent. These persons have discovered a "fit." Their many selves are not merely separate; they also "fit" together in some way. It may not be the same "fit" all the time. In fact, it may rarely be the exact same "fit." There is no ideal "fit" or mold that people should squeeze into. Rather, people are involved in a process of self-relatedness, a process that is ongoing and dynamic. They are always seeking and trying and changing in different situations, and yet they are stable and confident.

Incongruence

Such stability and confidence, however, are not always our experience. Often, I might be unaware of my experience, unaware of what I am thinking or feeling or doing. At another time or place, I might be aware of my experience but not communicating it, or unable to do so. At such times, I experience incongruence. I am not totally related with myself.

Another experience of incongruence is the example of the young woman described above. Her experience included an overawareness of one particular self to the exclusion of other selves. Such an experience might be described as a fixation in one of the many selves who I am. A fixation may appear as congruence or integration, and there may be times when it feels quite comfortable. But it may also be a repression of all but one of our many possible selves. When this is the case, people, sad to say, cannot experience themselves in a dynamic manner. They are caught. Most tragic, they are often unaware of their fixation even though they may be aware of some unidentified uneasiness. Thus the experience of incongruency can be found at two levels: the inability to relate our many selves and/or the unawareness of the unrelated condition.

I will conclude this discussion of relatedness with self by sharing an Hasidic tale that touches me deeply in its challenge. An Hasid in Eastern Europe committed himself to fasting from food and drink from one Sabbath to the next. By Friday afternoon at the end of the week, the Hasid had become thirsty. So, when he saw some water he went to it and readied himself to drink. But, instantly, he realized that he would be breaking his commitment and that it was close to the end of the week-long fast. So he did not drink. But then, a few moments later, he felt proud that he had overcome the temptation. Now, aware of this pride, he argued with himself that it would be better to drink the water and break the commitment than to fall prey to pride. The man then returned to the water. He was just about to drink it when . . . he noticed that he was no longer thirsty. A while later the Sabbath began, and the Hasid entered the house of his teacher. As he crossed the threshold, the teacher said to him: "Patchwork."[3]

This man had overcome his temptation to break his fast and his temptation to pride. Why, then, did his teacher treat him so harshly? According to Martin Buber, the object of the teacher's reproof was the wavering quality of the man's action. The work was not all of a piece. It was not done entirely from a related heart.

The purpose of formal meditation has often been presented as being discovery — the enterprise of discovering the heart of oneself, discovering an integration of the many selves who are in the heart, the center of these selves. But discovery does not take place only in formal meditation; it is built into the life process of each person. Formal meditation may be a great aid to it, but the process itself is meditative or prayerful even when it is not recognized in a formal manner.

So far, the focus in this chapter has been on self-relatedness. But this is only one aspect of the task in which we are involved, the task of recognizing and actualizing our network of relations. Another aspect of human relatedness has to do with other human persons.

Creative Spaces

On both the popular and professional levels, there are numerous books and articles and workshops that deal with interpersonal relationships. The development of these relationships is central to the whole matter of relatedness with others. The repairing of broken relationships is a key concern in this process of development. Another key concern is the realizing of relationships that have never been recognized. My concern here will be with only a few of the elements of this complex network of interpersonal relationships.

In general, relatedness with others involves finding connections with other people. But it also involves finding the spaces between oneself and other persons. A Chinese Taoist story illustrates the point:

There was a butcher who butchered for over fifty years without ever sharpening his knives. Finally, someone asked the butcher why he didn't need to sharpen his knives. The butcher responded by explaining that meat is solid, but that it also contains interstices or spaces. He pointed out that when he cut the meat he did so by passing the knife through the interstices. Hence, there was no resistance, no obstacle for the knife to overcome. That is why the knives remained sharp.[4]

The butcher was skilled enough to find the spaces. And that is what we do — find the spaces — when we actualize the interpersonal relationships embedded in our network of relations.

Another story, from the Hasidic tradition, points in the same direction:

> Rabbi Abraham was asked: "Our sages say: 'And there is not a thing that has not its place.' And so man too has his own place. Then why do people sometimes feel so crowded?" He replied: "Because each wants to occupy the place of another."[5]

To be related with another person means, among other things, that we give the person space to be unique. We do not try to control, and we are not a parasite on the person. We allow the person to occupy his or her own place.

Karl Rahner suggests something similar in reference to unity in the Church. He says that the only thing that will bring unity on the human level is love of others that is deep enough to allow others to be different.[6] I would add that the differences we must allow are not only the ones between persons; we must also allow differences a person may have within himself or herself. Another Hasidic story illustrates this point. The story refers to God, but I believe it also is significant for interpersonal relations.

> A disciple asked the Baal-Shem: "Why is it that one who clings to God and knows he is close to him sometimes experiences a sense of interruption and remoteness?" The Baal-Shem explained: "When a father sets out to teach his little son to walk, he

stands in front of him and holds his two hands on either side of the child, so that he cannot fall, and the boy goes toward his father between his father's hands. But the moment he is close to his father, the father moves away a little, and holds his hands farther apart, and he does this over and over, so that the child may learn to walk.[7]

With a few changes in appropriate places, this story could also be about a deep friendship. The persons involved recognize the connections and affinity between themselves. But they are also conscious of each other's uniqueness, each other's need to be truly other in order for the relationship to be truly mutual.

Destructive Spaces

Up to this point I have indicated the creative side of the spaces between people. There are moments, however, when a relationship becomes strained. The connecting lines in the network become tight and tense. The space, now, does not enable the connection; it manifests unease or anxiety or anger — a disturbance of the relation.

What must be done? What can be done? What do I want to do?

One possibility is to pull away from the relationship, to imagine that it does not exist. Sometimes, when the personal sanity of the people involved is at stake, this is all that can be done. When this is the case, it would seem better not to repress the relationship; it would seem better to face the fact that it cannot develop further, that the distance between the persons is too great and too treacherous for either to navigate.

One hope, however, does exist: the people involved can try to keep an eye open for possible bridges that might arise *accidentally*. (The people involved may feel too hurt and too vulnerable to risk taking a deliberate first step.)

A second possibility is for one of the parties to give in. On the positive side, this might release the strain for the persons involved. But on the negative side, it would also mean that one person is now under the control of the other. Hence, while one strain is relaxed another begins to develop.

A third possibility comes to fore when at least one of the persons continuously seeks to ease the strain by risking communication. When this happens, the strain is clarified for both persons, and they can then seek a way to ease it.

A few other ways by which relatedness with others is blocked are stereotyping and the use of defense mechanisms. To stereotype another person is to define that person totally on a general basis — for example, in terms of the person's background, religion, race, or some other category. Stereotyping blocks relatedness by destroying a person's uniqueness. I can never be related with a person if I simply see him or her merely as a general type rather than as a particular person.

Another obstacle is known as defense mechanisms. Psychologists have often suggested that these defensive measures not only protect the self but also destroy an honest relationship. In general, people usually are not conscious of the fact that they are using defense mechanisms. I will briefly touch upon four such mechanisms that are widely used: rationalization, projection, reaction formation, and repression.

Rationalization involves giving a good reason for what I do — but not giving the real reason.

Projection takes place when I attribute to others, in some exaggerated form, bad qualities of my own that I do not even recognize in myself.

In *reaction formation,* a person tries to hide a motive or feeling or value by expressing, in very strong terms, the opposite motive or feeling or value.

Finally, a *repression* is the public denial of a personal impulse or tendency or wish that the person desires to keep in check.

Connections and Uniqueness

Relatedness with others is a dimension of our cosmotheandric network linking people, the world, and God. In the past few pages, I have touched on some of the creative and destructive spaces between people. But along with space, relatedness with others also involves being aware of and actualizing connections. This task of awareness and actualization begins when one person takes the risk of courageously addressing or responding to another person. When a connection is made, it has many of the qualities described in previous chapters — especially trust, wonder, and presence. Interconnectedness also involves mutuality, directness, sharing, caring, respecting, knowing the other, and responsibility. In other words, when there are no destructive spaces or connections, relatedness with another person continually develops the connections and spaces between the persons.

I will conclude this section with two quotes, one from Elie Wiesel and the other from Carl Rogers. Wiesel describes how a bridge can be built between persons when he writes:

> We are alone, but we are capable of communicating to one another both our loneliness and our desire to break through it. You say, "I'm alone." Someone answers, "I'm alone too." There's a shift in the scale of power. A bridge is thrown between the two abysses.[8]

On the other hand, Carl Rogers, comparing people to sunsets, affirms their uniqueness and his unwillingness to control their beauty:

> People are just as wonderful as sunsets, if I can let them be. In fact, perhaps the reason we can truly

appreciate a sunset is that we cannot control it. When I look at a sunset as I did the other evening I don't find myself saying, "soften the orange a little on the right hand corner, and put more purple along the base, and use a little more pink in the cloud color." I don't do that. I don't try to control a sunset. I watch it with awe as it unfolds.[9]

Each unique person is as wonderful as a sunset. No person should be controlled but allowed to unfold. Yet, at the same time, in our network of relations, people are connected; and we all need to recognize that the activity or inactivity of each one affects the others. What is unfolding is not simply the individual person; it is also the network of relations itself. Prayer as relatedness involves realizing and actualizing the network of relations in oneself and with others.

Earth — Ground of Our Life

There is a second major element of the cosmotheandric network, and that is — nature. When it comes to nature, relatedness is not only of the utmost necessity, it is axiomatic — simply the way things are.

Reality embraces not only relations among human beings but also between human beings and the rest of the natural universe. Appearances suggest that we are all separate from one another, and these appearances do not lie. But they also do not tell the whole truth. Not only am I, as a human being, born *into* the world. I am also born *out of* or *from* the world. My connection with the so-called outside world is an intrinsic connection. I breathe and the line of my breath is a lifeline within the cosmotheandric network of relations.

The ecological network is clearly expressed in the following story and commentary. It seems that an aquarium ran short of seawater just as it received a shipment of live saltwater creatures. Knowing the formula for salt water, the curators of the aquarium decided to manufacture some. When this task was completed, they put the creatures into the aquarium newly filled with their manufactured seawater. The creatures soon died. The curators now tried a new experiment: they added some real seawater to the manufactured water. Then they put some creatures into it. These creatures lived.

That experiment has these implications: the many drops of water in the great oceans comprise a life of their own, and this life in the drops of water makes possible the life of the creatures that live within it.

But this is not all. Our own human life is also dependent on the life of the oceans. Our life is linked in a basic way with that of the ocean. If the oceans died, the death knell for human beings and all other creatures would not be far behind. Ocean death would raise the temperature. The rise in temperature would melt the ice caps at the North and South Poles. And the melted ice caps would cause floods. Then there would be rainlessness, resulting in global drought and famine. A final effect would be loss of the oxygen supply.

The connection between the human and the cosmic is intimate. And relatedness with nature is as important as relatedness with ourselves and with other human beings.

The Gospel According to Matthew tells us that we human beings are the salt of the earth. This comment points to our relation with the cosmos. Salt is a condiment that draws out the flavor of food; human beings can draw the flavor out of the earth. By reason of human consciousness, the cosmos becomes conscious of itself.

However, we must also realize that the earth is the necessary ground of our life. Prayer as relatedness not only involves ourselves and others, it is also an ecological enterprise. Having some power to manipulate the lands and the seas, we human beings must also be aware of the intrinsic network of relations

— relations that exist among the various natural elements as well as between ourselves and nature.

Prayer as relatedness includes nature. It is wonderful and awesome, this prayer. Hopefully, it will arise out of and lead to a relation that transcends manipulation. These are some of the implications of the meditative walk in the woods or the contemplative sojourn by the sea.

The Divine Dimension

A third element of the cosmotheandric network is the divine. This element is both the root and the term of the other elements. It is their context and their horizon. They do not exist without it. Nor does the divine exist without the human and the cosmic.

What is the significance of the divine dimension? In this dimension each human person can experience the unmeasurable depth of his or her being. Each person can also experience the inexhaustible complexity of the network of relations in which we live. That network is not experienced simply as premade and unchangeable but as everchanging and everchangeable. No person, no element, no dimension of the network is a merely closed being. Living in the network, we are continuously touched by other elements. We are more than the particular and private aspects of our lives. There is always more than meets the eye or touches the heart. It is this "evermore" character of life in the network that I refer to as the divine dimension of the cosmotheandric network of relations.

This depth dimension is present both in the human and in the cosmic dimensions. It is also present in the relations among these dimensions. The divine dimension, however, is not the center of the network. In a very real sense, each point of the network — in all three dimensions: cosmic, human, and divine — can be conceived of as a center. God is, as it were, in need of the cosmic and the human as they are in need of God.

Usually, when one is speaking of prayer, it is relatedness with God that is emphasized. Yet, if I focus only on that dimension I might miss the entire network. In fact, I would suggest that we will miss the divine dimension if we try to focus on it alone; the focus would eliminate the other dimensions within which we recognize the divine.

To pursue the depth of my relation with myself, with other people, and with the cosmos is to pursue the depth of reality which is God. To stop short of this depth is to stop short of relatedness within the cosmotheandric network. It is to ignore a central dimension of reality: the "evermore" of the dynamic exchange among the various dimensions in which we live and change and die.

In conclusion, I would like to share a bit more of the story of the Little Prince, with its power to manifest the power of relatedness. The Prince had become a close friend of a fox. After the two had become intimate, they had to separate. It was then that the fox shared a secret with the Prince. He said to him: "It is only with the heart that one can see rightly: what is essential is invisible to the eye."[10]

To see rightly, I would suggest, is to see relatedly. It is to see in the context of the ties that are a part of our life in the network. It is to see in the light of the spaces between the elements of the network. This is illustrated by a conversation between the Little Prince and the fox about "taming." What does it mean — to tame? Pointing out that taming is an act too often neglected, the fox said that taming means to establish ties. It was while their own ties to each other were being established that the Prince and the fox became increasingly aware of their uniqueness, of the creative spaces between them.[11]

To be related in a continuous life process is to realize and establish the ties as well as the spaces in which each of us is involved. Unless prayer happens in this context, it lacks its heart. The cosmotheandric network is the context of prayer. And prayer is the vibrant dynamism of the network itself.

Notes

1. I have placed this chapter here, rather than at the beginning of the book, because I preferred to share with the reader some of the more familiar aspects of the human roots of prayer before presenting the less familiar vision of reality suggested in this chapter.

2. I am deeply indebted to Raimundo Panikkar for his fundamental cosmotheandric intuition. This intuition is extensively described in his essay, "Colligite Fragmenta: For an Integration of Reality," which may be found in *From Alienation to Atoneness* edited by Francis A. Eigo (Villanova: Villanova University Press, 1977), p. 19ff. In 1974 I heard Panikkar deliver an address that became the basis for this essay. His address helped me to integrate insights I had gathered through reading and conversation.

3. Martin Buber, *Hasidism and Modern Man* (New York: Harper Torchbook, 1966), pp. 146-147.

4. Thomas Merton, *The Way of Chuang-Tzu* (New York: New Directions, 1965), pp. 45-47.

5. Martin Buber, *Tales of the Hasidim: The Later Masters* (New York: Schocken, 1948), p. 72.

6. Cf. Karl Rahner, *The Dynamic Element in the Church* (New York: Herder and Herder, 1964), p. 74.

7. Martin Buber, *Tales of the Hasidim: The Early Masters,* (New York: Schocken, 1947), p. 65.

8. Elie Wiesel, *The Gates of the Forest* (New York: Avon, 1967), p. 178.

9. Carl Rogers, "Some Elements of Effective Interperson Communication." The source of this article is unknown to me. Its content, however, is very much in accord with Roger's other writings.

10. Antoine de Saint-Exupery, *The Little Prince* (New York: Harcourt, Brace and World, 1943), p. 70.

11. Ibid., pp. 65-66.

7

Prayer as Perceptiveness

Being in Touch

A prayerful person is a person who is rooted in the cosmotheandric network of relations. Prayer involves both the
realization and actualization of that network in the forms of
questioning, wonder, silence, and concentration. Each of these
human experiences is grounded, to some degree, in the human
ability to perceive. Thus a perceptive person is a prayerful
person. The traditional forms of meditation and contemplation
profoundly affect a person's perception of reality.

In this chapter I am not going to discuss all the scientific,
physiological, psychological, and sociological findings about
perception. I will, rather, draw the broad lines of what it means
to be a perceptive person. By doing this, I will suggest that a
person's development in perceptiveness is also development in
prayerfulness.

Who, then, is a perceptive person? The response to this
question will enable us to uncover how perceptiveness is prayerfulness. In general, a perceptive person is a person who is "in
touch with" himself or herself — and with the cosmos — and
with God. That is, the perceptive person is "in contact with"

the cosmotheandric network in which we live and of which we are a fundamental dimension.

The image of "touch" is very powerful and sensuous. It is used here, initially, to refer to all our senses: sight, hearing, tasting, smelling, and, of course, touching. Hence, it is sensuous. "Touch" is powerful insofar as it points to a double movement of each human person and hence to a dual operation in perceptivity. This dual operation involves both a "taking in" of impressions and a "giving out" of expressions.

"Touch," then, is impressive. When a person is "in touch," that person feels or "takes in" something. "Touch" is also expressive. It is a person's moving beyond himself or herself to share with another. Perceptiveness, as being "in touch," is, then, an operation by which life flows through our fundamental network of relations. To be a perceptive person is to be alive, to be impressive (to take in, to receive), and to be expressive (to put out, to give).

The Receptive Dimension

A common understanding of perceptiveness focuses on its receptive character. This insight is expressed in the many words used to describe a perceptive person. Such a person is observant, open, tuned in, a good listener. The perceptive person recognizes or "picks up" the feelings of others, notices small changes, has all his or her antennae out. This person "picks up" or "takes in" sense impressions and the moods or feelings these impressions suggest. Thus, the perceptive person is not only sympathetic but empathetic — "in touch" with the heart of the other.

"The other" refers both to other people and to nature. A perceptive person is able to listen to and to hear another — to "take in" that other. However, the process of "taking in" is not symbiotic; the other is allowed to be other. The spaces are recognized and respected. A perceptive person does not imagine the other as a projection of self; the other is seen not on self's terms but on the other's terms. The perceptive person is in touch with self but not centered on self. This person is able to go beyond self toward the other, to receive the other, allowing the other to remain other while also remaining oneself. The receptivity involved in perceptiveness includes both identification and separation.

A few stories will illustrate some of the dynamics just described. A university professor once inquired about Zen. He was received by a Zen master who immediately served tea. The master poured the professor's cup full and, then, kept on pouring. The professor watched this and exclaimed: "Stop! It's already full. No more will go in." The master replied: "You are like this cup, full of your own ideas and opinions. How can I show you Zen unless you first empty your cup?"[1]

The perceptive person is one with an empty cup, a person who is able to receive with freshness and newness. One effect of Zen meditation is the emptying of the cup, the change of perception by which a person's own concepts and ideas do not get into the way of relation with another.

In an Hasidic story we are told that the great Maggid of Mezritch once said to his disciples: "I shall teach you the best way to say Torah. You must cease to be aware of yourselves. You must be nothing but an ear which hears what the universe of the word is constantly saying within you. The moment you start hearing what you yourself are saying, you must stop."[2]

A perceptive person listens to the other as the Hasidic disciple is called upon to listen to Torah.

Another story. The delightful Sufi, Nasrudin, went to see a rich man and asked: "Give me some money." The rich man replied, "Why?" Nasrudin said: "I want to buy an elephant." The rich man said: "If you have no money, you can't afford to keep an elephant." "I came here," said Nasrudin, "to get money, not advice."[3]

Unlike the rich man, a perceptive person listens to and hears only what is said. We can become perceptive by emptying our cup, listening to the other, and hearing only what is said.

The Expressive Dimension

However, if we stop here, we will have only a partial understanding of perceptiveness — its receptive dimension, its impressiveness. A perceptive person is also expressive; our senses not only receive impressions but also give or "put out" expressions.

There are two ways of expression inherent in perceptiveness. The first way is response: a perceptive person not only notices the moods or changes in others but also gives expression, verbally or nonverbally, to what is noticed. This response may simply reflect what is perceived or "seen." For example, if you perceive that someone is overjoyed, you may simply respond to that person's manifest joy. But on another occasion, you might notice that a friend is overwrought about a separation and cannot deal with the feelings it involves. Here your response would be more complex; you would have to consider not only the painful feeling of separation but also the inability to face these feelings. My basic point here is simply that perceptiveness shows itself both in receptivity *and* in responsiveness.

But there is a second way by which expression is inherent in perceptiveness: a perceptive person shows who he or she is in the process of responding. This way of expression is partially described by Bernard Lonergan when he writes:

Our perceiving is not just a function of the impressions made on our senses. It has an orientation of its own and it selects, out of a myriad of others, just those impressions that can be constructed into a pattern with meaning.[4]

86

What we select to "see" says something about who we are. Perceptiveness is not simply passive. It is also active. We perceive according to who we are. Perceptiveness is expressive of our identity. Our flesh and bones, our bodies, are powerful symbols, and our senses are part of this bodily symbol. Our "looking" not only "takes in" what we see but also manifests something about us — for example, the fact that we are intense or relaxed or anxious. Besides selecting what we receive, we express the way we are.

In summary, perceptiveness is a cybernetic process involving both a "taking in" and a "putting out," receiving and responding, impressing and expressing. Unless both of these elements are operative, perception is blocked. The perceptive person is an open and responsive person and hence a "caring" person. He or she is a person who is "in touch" with self and with others — people and nature. This person's part of the network of relations is alive and pulsing.

Two Examples

In conclusion, I will share with you the dilemmas that two friends of mine have experienced, dilemmas that manifest the "balance" between impression and expression in perceptiveness. One friend was confronted with the reality of a totally free summer — three months without any demands or formal responsibilities. Before the summer began, he recognized both the possibilities and the dangers in this situation and took steps to deal with them. One danger was that of too much leisure, too much unscheduled time, and the possibility of boredom. In response to that, he planned his days in such a way that life would not just happen to him. But he also planned the summer in such a way that he would not be bound by a rigorous structure.

What does all this have to do with perceptiveness? Besides the fact that he recognized his situation, it has this to do with it: if he had simply let life happen, there would have been too little input; he would have become lazy and unreceptive. Without such input, his output would have been less. Instead, he planned a "free schedule" in which perceptiveness was allowed to grow both through impression and expression.

Another friend is experiencing the opposite problem — too much input, too little leisure. As a teacher, student, and single parent, she is continuously bombarded with input, impressions that call for responses. At the same time, she knows very well that she does not have enough time for all that she wants to do and express of herself. Aware of these limitations, she wonders if there is any way she can be the person she knows she is. This person is dealing with this dilemma. She does it by planning her life so that her perceptiveness can be a bit less "unbalanced." In the midst of the continual input and response, she keeps an eye open for moments of refreshment and revitalization. How she does this I will discuss further on in this chapter.

Conscious Sensitivity

Up to this point I have tried to confine myself to the operation of perceptiveness as impressive and expressive. Two aspects of perceptiveness have been in my mind and implicit in the above discussion: sensitivity and awareness. In every discussion I had about perceptiveness, while in the process of writing this chapter, these two words were central. I would ask a person what he or she thought was characteristic of a perceptive person. Almost universally and immediately, the response would include sensitivity and awareness.

A perceptive person is a sensitive person, that is, a person whose senses are open and available to a great variety and subtleness of impressions and expressions. Such sensitivity is not necessarily accompanied by awareness or consciousness of what is sensed. When this awareness is not present, the sensitivity by itself is not yet perceptiveness. A perceptive person is a *consciously* sensitive person.

A Zen story may enable this idea about perceptiveness to become clearer. There was a blind man who lived near Bankei's temple. When Bankei died, the blind man told a friend: "Since I am blind, I cannot watch a person's face, so I must judge his character by the sound of his voice. Ordinarily, when I hear someone congratulate another upon his happiness or success, I also hear a secret tone of envy. When condolence is expressed for the misfortune of another, I hear pleasure and satisfaction, as if the one condoling was really glad there was something left to gain in his own world. In all my experience, however, Bankei's voice was always sincere. Whenever he expressed happiness, I heard nothing but happiness, and whenever he expressed sorrow, sorrow was all I heard."[5]

The focal point of this story is Bankei's purity of expression — his perceptiveness. I would also call attention to the perceptiveness of the blind man. His senses were keen. His discrimination was subtle. He was aware of what he sensed, and could describe it. He was a consciously sensitive person, that is, a perceptive person. Both the blind man and Bankei are "poor in spirit" in Meister Eckhart's understanding of this phrase: "To be poor in spirit is to be sensitive to other spirits."[6] Such sensitivity is conscious.

A Given and a Task

How can a person become perceptive? In general, I do not believe that anyone is fully perceptive. Hence, growth in perceptiveness is a lifelong task — at times a joy and at other times a burden, even a painful one. However, perceptiveness is not only a task. It is also, to some extent, a "given." It is on this "given" quality of perceptiveness that I will first focus.

Each person is born into the world at a certain time, in a

certain place, within a particular culture and socioeconomic condition. The person is then educated in accord with this culture and condition. Education is precisely a training in perceptiveness, a schooling in conscious sensitivity. In fact, one of my friends describes perceptiveness as "schooled observance." This is training not only of the mind but also of the senses — for example, the eye of a painter, the ear of a musician, the smell and taste of a cook, the touch of a potter. Such schooling can be "taken in" technically and/or creatively.

Technical learning involves "taking in" a way of sensing, plus an awareness of this way of sensing. It also involves an exact imitating of the process to the point where the process becomes "second nature." Creative learning involves "taking in" exactly the same "data" as in technical learning with one major difference: creative training further develops one's conscious sensitivity or perceptiveness.

Merely technical learning can be a great advantage at times — for example, when a person is without the physical or emotional resources to operate at full potential. But, at the same time, a person engaged only at the technical level can stagnate and become unperceptive, bound into a systematic understanding of reality.

Perceptiveness can be lost or destroyed by conditions such as sickness, forgetfulness, ignorance, or exhaustion. But it is possible for a person to take care so that his or her perceptiveness will not be destroyed. Such care also enables a person's perception to deepen and broaden, to become more subtle.

One of my friends is a teacher in a city high school. She is one of the few people I know who absolutely enjoys teaching in a high school. Many demands are made on her sensitivity. In class, she continuously tries to discover her students' moods, feelings, thought patterns, and insights. Then she responds to what she discovers. An exhausting day! A few years ago, she and her husband decided to build a home away from the city.

They bought a wooded property and designed their home to be part of these woods. One room in the home is hers; it has windows on three sides and can be used for work or relaxation or leisure. My friend describes her home as an aesthetic environment which she needs to give her own senses a time and a place to operate. I would also suggest that it is a place where she can care for her perceptiveness in both its dimensions — impression and expression.

The care of perceptiveness, however, cannot depend on a person's socioeconomic conditions. The friend I spoke of a few pages back — the person with no leisure time — is a case in point. She does not have the same financial resources as my friend the high-school teacher. And she has constant demands on her time; her life is exhausting. So what does she do? She continually studies her situation in its details, identifying commitments or duties and pinpointing where she is most needy. Once she has focused on her areas of need, she asks what options are available to her. She then "tries on" the options, mentally and/or actually, in order to discover which ones are viable. Once she has reached her conclusion, she structures or plans the viable options into her week. These options become sacred. For example, she will set aside a time to wash her hair once during the week. Or she will try to read undisturbed, or watch a lighted candle quietly in a dark room, or listen to a record all the way through. The times and places for these options are set up — everyone in her family is told — and those times and places and options are sacred. Over the course of weeks or months, the options change, depending on the needs. However, the process of caring for her perceptiveness goes on. She has made a conscious, planned decision and effort to become refreshed.

The importance I place on the two examples just described is not on what is done; the specific activities are unique for each person. The reason I went into detail is to express the importance of caring for one's perceptiveness. Such care is continuously necessary for a person to be consciously sensitive. It is not selfish or self-centered. It is, rather, manifestative of a concern for the network in which we live.

Spontaneity and Zest

Perceptiveness is not only the result of training, it is also spontaneous and zestful. (In the next chapter I will suggest that perceptiveness is also graceful. Thus, to say that it is the result of "training" is somewhat misleading.) The following Hasidic story about Rabbi Moshe Leib begins to suggest what I mean here.

One midnight while the rabbi was absorbed in his mystical readings, he heard a rap on his window. He went to the door, where he found a drunken peasant who asked for shelter and a bed for the night. For a moment the rabbi's heart was angry. He said to himself: "How can a drunk have the insolence to ask to be let in, and what business has he in this house?" But then he silently thought in his heart: "And what business has he in God's world? If God gets along with him, can I reject him?" He opened the door at once and prepared a bed.

The rabbi was spontaneous. It took him only a moment to break out of his original interpretation of the situation and to perceive it with new eyes. A perceptive person who is spontaneous perceives the situation with a "beginner's mind," as if for the first time, with freshness. Yet, at the same time, the perception is grounded in training. The rabbi believed in God; and his belief, nurtured by prayer and study, affected all his perceptions.

Often, a belief can confine a person's perceptiveness. This is what initially happened to the rabbi. He had a stereotype about drunks. But that belief was challenged by his belief in God, and he then perceived the situation differently and spontaneously.

A second quality of a perceptive person is zest. A zestful person is a live person, a person who can taste the essence of a situation, who can feel deeply the flavor of an impression or an expression. In the hands of a zestful person, a situation becomes alive. The network is animated. It is sensed and known. It becomes contagious.

Perceptive persons are spontaneous and zestful. They are not bound by the patterns of training or socialization they have undergone. They are able to make new connections and savor them. They are thoughtfully spontaneous and responsibly zestful. Jesus gave expression to this spirit when he declared that he had come that we might have life and have it to the full.

Furthermore, I would describe the perceptive people as artists. By artists, I do not mean people who paint portraits or landscapes or write poems or sculpt madonnas. Rather, I mean "ordinary" people whose lives are artistic. These people plunge into the everyday where we live and open it up by word or silence, movement or stillness. Perceptive persons live life both artfully and artlessly.

In summary, perceptiveness is a human operation within the cosmotheandric network of relations, an operation that puts a person "in touch" with the other elements and dimensions of the network. It involves impressions and expressions that are consciously sensitive. It is the way a person enters into the heart of the world. A prayerful person is a person who is open to that heart and, in this openness, touches upon the mystery that is God, the cosmos, and the human. Daniel Berrigan, describing how the world confronted him with questions and refused to give him answers, wrote:

Infinitely better than answers, the world showed me
its heart. Slowly, subtly, with infinite compassion
for my ignorance, it led me into the inner rhythms of
human existence, the tides of fury and lust and fear
and heartbreaking nobility which are its secret. I
rode these tides. I learned (how slowly, with what

resistance) that I was no priest until I consented, in those waters, to be a human being.[7]

Berrigan affirms a growth of perceptiveness, an unfolding of a secret. To pray is to search out that secret and to embrace it, and then to be able to let it go in the further pursuit of the secret, the mystery. Such a prayer is the simple gaze at truth which Thomas Aquinas calls contemplation.

According to the Sufi, Hujwiri, such a prayer is of the essence of sainthood. Hujwiri affirms that holiness "consists in seeing the things as they are — in being a seer."[8] To be a seer is to be able "to see," which is to be perceptive. And this is no easy task or condition for us to pursue.

> One of the boys at Nasrudin's school asked: "Which was the greatest achievement, that of the man who conquered an empire, the man who could have but did not, or the man who prevented another from doing so?"
>
> "I don't know about any of that," said Nasrudin, "but I do know a more difficult task than any of those."
>
> "What is that?"
>
> "Trying to teach you to see things as they really are."[9]

Notes

1. Paul Reps, *Zen Flesh, Zen Bones* (New York: Anchor), p. 3.
2. Martin Buber, *Tales of Hasidim: The Early Masters* (New York: Schocken, 1947), p. 107.
3. Idries Shah, *The Pleasantries of the Incredible Mulla Nasrudin* (New York: Dutton, 1971), p. 13.
4. Bernard Lonergan, *Method in Theology* (New York: Herder and Herder, 1972), p. 59.

5. Paul Reps, *Zen Flesh, Zen Bones,* p. 30.
6. Raymond B. Blakney, trans., *Meister Eckhart* (New York: Harper Torchbook, 1941), p. 53.
7. Daniel Berrigan, *The World Showed Me Its Heart* (St. Louis, Missouri: National Sodality Service, 1966), p. 10.
8. Masaud Farzan, *The Tale of the Reed Pipe* (New York: Dutton, 1974), pp. 65-66.
9. Idries Shah, *The Pleasantries of the Incredible Mulla Nasrudin,* p. 133.

8

Prayer as Grace

Mystery of Grace and Effort

Persons who attempt to develop their perceptiveness and concentration can tell us that much hard work is involved in the process. The same can be said for prayer. But hard work is not the whole story. For prayer is also grace, a gift. It happens when we least expect it.

When it does happen, there may be a feeling of having "let go." Prayer is the coming to surface of the mystery of God and the world and human beings. It cannot just be conjured up at will. As Saint Paul points out, no one can really say, "Lord, Lord," unless he is moved by the Spirit of God. It is said from one's heart, which is the heart of the world, the Silence who is the Father — Abba.

Prayer as grace is the grace that is realized in the midst of life. It involves the realization that I cannot control another person's responses or reactions to my words or actions. I do not even entirely control my own responses and reactions. Not all depends on me. I can do what I am able to or what I must do, but what happens involves the responses of other people as well as events of which I am unaware. To live in a network of relations is to recognize that I am not self-sufficient.

A deep mystery is present in this fact. It is a mystery that has wracked the minds and hearts of numerous people from many ages and cultures. It is the mystery of grace and effort.

The Gospel According to Mark tells a story about a woman who suffered with a hemorrhage for twelve years. The woman had undergone much painful treatment under a variety of doctors, but all these efforts had failed. This woman had heard about Jesus, and one day she approached him. She touched his clothes, believing that she would be cured, and the source of the bleeding dried up at that moment. This is grace.

Much effort is put into the tilling of the soil and the planting of a field. A farmer works to guarantee growth. He does all he can. But the growth is not entirely up to him. The weather, the quality of the soil, and many other factors are beyond his control. The farmer realizes the intimate connections of the network of relations. All the factors work for the growth of the seeds. This is grace.

A dancer strives for years to concentrate his or her energies, to develop form and movement. A time comes, possibly, when he or she dances seemingly without effort. The body flows in the rhythm of the music. It looks to us as if he or she does not strain at all. The dancer is graceful. This is grace.

"Think of the flowers; they never have to spin or weave; yet, I assure you, not even Solomon in all his regalia was robed like one of these. . . . But you, you must not set your hearts on things to eat and things to drink; nor must you worry." (Luke 12:27,29) This passage may seem to be utterly fatalistic. Yet, it is quite expressive of grace. Each human person is unique. Each is precious. This is grace. The phrase "nor must you worry" is also expressive of grace. Not to worry is not the same as being unconcerned, nor does it mean that one does not plan. It simply points to the fact that neither the past, the present, nor the future are entirely the doing of one person or condition. Again, this is grace.

Interplay

The interplay of grace and effort is also quite evident in friendship. There is nothing that one can do to guarantee the establishment of a friendship. I can work at a relationship and hope that it will develop into friendship. The working at the friendship is the effort. It is bringing myself to a relationship with whatever resources may be at my command and those that may spontaneously arise from my being. I cannot, however, determine the response of the other person. For me, this other's response is grace. I can trust another person, and this trust may or may not lead to friendship. But I cannot force another to trust me. That trust of me is grace.

The interplay between grace and effort is developed in a unique manner in the Chinese attitude called *wei-wu-wei,* which can be translated as "doing without doing." Both elements are present here: effort is the "doing," and grace is the "not doing." The Chinese sage Chuang Tzu gives expression to this attitude:

> Heaven does nothing: its nondoing is its serenity. Earth does nothing: its nondoing is its rest. From the union of these two nondoings all actions proceed, all things are made. How vast, how invisible this coming-to-be! All things come from nowhere! How vast, how invisible — no way to explain it! All beings in their perfection are born of nondoing. Hence, it is said: "Heaven and earth do nothing, yet there is nothing they do not do." Where is the man who can attain this nondoing?[1]

This man is the archer who, when he shoots for no gain, has all his skill. But when he shoots for a prize, he is divided. His skill has not changed, but he thinks more of winning than of shooting his bow.[2]

Shooting demands effort. There is effort in "nondoing." There is also grace in "doing." When the effort is not divided, this is graceful effort. Again, this does not mean that there is no concern. To be concerned is to enter a situation with all the resources that are available. "Nondoing" is allowing the situation to have its input. This is effortful grace, that is, allowing the effort of all involved to come into play. Thus concern is also grace, my concern and your concern.

The integration of grace and effort is also very prominent in play. To play is to give oneself over to the game without being *overly* concerned about the outcome. It is to play the game with all one's strength and skill and, yet, to lose oneself in it at the same time. The game has a structure, but not so much structure that we are bound or hemmed in. The structure depends more or less on the game. Its purpose is to allow the free play of one's strength and energies; to let these energies become concentrated so that body and spirit can move with each other; to let them "play into" each other. There is effort and there is grace.

Prayer, especially worship or liturgy, may be compared to play. Liturgy is work — "work for the community," in its original Greek meaning. Yet, it is also a work in which people can lose themselves. When this liturgy arises from the Silence which is at its root, when it is expressive of the cosmotheandric network, it then becomes the worship in spirit and in truth of which John the Evangelist speaks (John 4:23-24). It is graceful.

Flow

Closely related to the playful aspect of gracefulness is its character of "flow." A recent psychological study has suggested that activities are fun or rewarding in themselves because of their quality of "flow."[3] The image of "flow" reminds me of a river and its movement. The water is channeled by the banks of the river. These banks do not simply confine the water; they give it a structure for its movement, as do the rules of a game. The river moves smoothly. It flows.

When this image of "flow" is applied to human activity, it points to the smoothness of that activity. A writer is said to flow when there is a smooth integration of thought, feeling, and expression within the freeing structure of language. A perceptive person flows when impression and expression are integrated.

The cosmotheandric network of relations flows when the spaces and connections are respected and integrated. The opposite of "flowing" is "awkward." Thus, at times, we meet up with "awkward" literary constructions. During the many weeks a child is learning to walk, the child's movement progresses from awkward to flowing. After many more years the flow might become graceful, that is, flow without any awkwardness.

What makes flow to be flow? In a previous chapter, I spoke of finding the spaces in the network of relations. To flow is to move "in the spaces" without bumping into something or someone (both physically or psychologically). The person who flows is very aware and sensitive, that is, perceptive. Yet, such perceptiveness, in its awareness aspect, is not an obstacle to flow. It is an unselfconscious awareness. The awareness extends to the entire situation rather than to one's self alone. Thus unselfconscious awareness includes self-awareness, not as isolated from the whole network but as integrated within it. Flow is flow because of this kind of awareness which unselfconsciously finds the spaces.

A person can be trained to flow, but such training does not necessarily result in flow. Flow is grace. Thus, a person can be shown the various movements necessary for swimming. The person can then practice these movements for hours until, suddenly, swimming becomes a joy. All the movements begin to work together with the water. The swimmer flows. The flow has taken effort, but is finally the "result" of grace and effort.

Another example is learning to ride a bicycle. The learner strives to maintain balance while coordinating bodily movements with the bicycle. After many attempts, balance is found. This is grace. The rider now flows.

In both of these examples, the flow is related to the discovery of coordination. Imagine all the bodily muscles that must be coordinated in swimming or bicycle riding. We may be aware of some of these movements while we make the effort to coordinate them, but we are never totally aware of all the movements. Once they all begin to work together, we begin to flow. Grace has happened.

Thus, gracefulness involves "flow," an unselfconscious coordination within a person and of the person with the other elements in the situation. Anne Morrow Lindbergh's suggestion about grace is close to this. She writes that "by grace I mean an inner harmony, essentially spiritual, which can be translated into an outward harmony."[4] To this I would add: not only is the harmony spiritual, it is also natural. It is the diversity in unity of the cosmotheandric network.

Unconditional Acceptance

Another aspect of grace is that it is unconditioned. It does not depend entirely on anyone or anything. It is lavish. The parable of the gracious father in Luke 15 gives expression to this dimension of grace. The father graciously welcomes his wandering son home. The son had left home with his inheritance, so the father does not have to welcome him back as a member of the household. But the father does welcome his son, and his welcome is not conditioned by any requirements. It is simply a gracious welcome.

This grace is also called forgiveness. It involves freely lifting the burden of the past from someone's shoulders, even from one's own shoulders. It involves seeing that, behind what appears, there is unconditional acceptance — of another or of oneself — the loving of a person even when the person is not understood. Here grace is not merely some thing. People are grace for other people.

All that has been said to this point about grace is prayerful. It may seem to be an impossible ideal. My point is that it is not an impossible ideal but a dimension of the very fabric of life. Life is effort and life is grace. Grace and effort are so interrelated in life that the very effort is graced.

The paradox of grace and effort is not solved. It cannot be solved as a mathematical equation. Rather, it is lived out in the changing life situations of each person. To pray is to be able to enter into these situations, into the network. Prayer is the living of these situations. In this way, it is of the essence of action and at the center of the active life. When lived, my action becomes my prayer and my prayer becomes my action. For, to "pray always" as Paul recommends, is to live in the mystery we call life. Prayer involves the courage to meet each call from this cosmotheandric mystery.

Notes

1. Thomas Merton, *The Way of Chuang Tzu* (New York: New Directions, 1965), pp. 101-102.
2. Ibid., p. 107.
3. Cf. William B. Furlong, "The Fun in Fun," *Psychology Today* (June, 1976), p. 35ff.
4. Anne Morrow Lindbergh, *Gift from the Sea* (New York: Pantheon, 1955), p. 23.

9

Prayer as Wisdom

Wisdom — The Inner Connection

In the previous chapters we have viewed a variety of the human roots of the experience of prayer: questioning, wonder, silence, concentration, perceptiveness, and grace. Each of these experiences is grounded in the fertile soil of the cosmotheandric network of relations. In this final chapter, I would like to suggest that the intrinsic connection among these experiences is wisdom, and that the search for and expression of wisdom is prayer.

In the Book of Wisdom we read that the spirit of the Lord is wisdom, and that this spirit is "that which holds all things together." (Wisdom 1:7) We read further that wisdom is "an inexhaustible treasure to men, and those who acquire it win God's friendship." (Wisdom 7:14) The acquisition of wisdom is the realization of the divine dimension of the network of relations. It is also the way to realizing that dimension. Wisdom is the "goal" and the means to the "goal." Prayer is the term and the way to the term. The term and the goal, the way and the means, are identified in the cosmotheandric network.

What is wisdom? Wisdom is often associated with age — the wise old man or woman. However, wisdom is not restricted to the elderly. It can also be found in the young. It is my present task to attempt a description of wisdom.

In general, I cannot adequately describe wisdom. For wisdom, like prayer, can only be pointed to. It cannot be defined. In the chapter on speaking about prayer (chapter 1), I included Chuang Tzu's story about Duke Hwan of Khi and the wheelwright. The wheelwright spoke of the wisdom found in books as the dirt that the sages have left behind. The ancient wise people took their wisdom to the grave with them. What they left behind — the words — is merely dirt. That dirt, however, can be enlivened. It can become fertile soil. It itself may not be wisdom, but it may be able to point us to wisdom. This can happen when the words are taken to heart, when the words are taken into the reader and become part of that reader, when the words come alive again in a living, pulsing person. These words sometimes speak to a heart that is open to them because those words are the words which fit exactly into a situation. It is then that wisdom is born. Elie Wiesel suggests this when he writes:

> Sometimes it happens that we travel for a long time
> knowing that we have made the long journey solely
> to pronounce a certain word, a certain phrase, in a
> certain place. The meeting of the place and the word
> is a rare accomplishment on the scale of humanity.[1]

This meeting is wisdom.

The Wisdom of Jesus

Many words have been spoken in the praise of wisdom. They have been written in the Jewish and Christian Scriptures and in the sacred writings of the Orient. Today, when wisdom is often relegated to the Oriental guru, we forget that the teacher in Israel is a wise person. We forget that Jesus "grew in wisdom before God and man." In what does the wisdom of these sages consist? Where can it be found?

While wisdom, like prayer, is a gift, it also comes from

instruction and association with the wise. Wise persons arise in all the various religions as well as outside of formal religion. I will first speak of some of these wise persons, and then I will attempt to point to the nature of wisdom in their lives. At the same time I will be speaking of prayer. The wise person is a prayerful person.

In the Gospel According to Luke, we read that Jesus grew in wisdom and knowledge and love before God and man. (Luke 2:52) And Saint Paul speaks of the Christ as the wisdom of God. (1 Corinthians 1:24) With all the talk about Jesus as God or as human, as Savior or Redeemer, it is easy to forget that he is a wise person. What is it about Jesus that manifests his wisdom? He himself rarely speaks of wisdom. Only a few of his followers are presented in the Gospels as disciples of a sage. Thus, to discern his wisdom it is necessary to seek it in his manner of living. This style I would broadly categorize as wisely compassionate. It comes through to the reader of the Gospels in Jesus' various attitudes toward the many people he met.

Often Jesus was invited to dinner with the leaders of the town through which he was passing. One time he was invited to a meal in the home of a Pharisee called Simon. While they were at table, a woman entered the room and went to Jesus. She began to wash his feet with her tears and to dry them with her hair. Simon objected because of the bad reputation the woman had. Jesus responded with a parable which pointed to the heart of the situation:

> There was once a creditor who had two men in his debt; one owed him five hundred denarii, the other fifty. They were unable to pay, so he pardoned them both. Which of them will love him more? (Luke 7:41-42)

The Pharisee responded to Jesus' question by pointing out that the one who had been forgiven more would love more. Jesus confirmed this response. He did not condemn the Pharisee. Rather, he tried to let him come to an awareness of the issues involved, the heart of the situation. This is wisdom.

Many times Jesus was questioned by people he met. At times their questions were attempts to trick him. His responses were often such that the questions were thrown back at the inquirers; they were confronted with their own questions in terms of their own lives. An example of this is the dialogue between Jesus and the leaders about the woman taken in adultery. (John 8:1-11)

The same thing happened when a lawyer asked Jesus: "Who is my neighbor?" Jesus responded with the parable of the Good Samaritan and concluded by turning the question back to the lawyer. The real question is not, "Who is my neighbor?" but "To whom are you a neighbor?" (Luke 10:29-37)

A final example of Jesus' wisdom and compassion is the delightful story of Zacchaeus. Zacchaeus was a tax collector and, hence, a person not well received by the people whose taxes he collected. He had heard that Jesus was going to pass near his home, so he climbed a tree to get a better look. When Jesus saw Zacchaeus, he saw into his heart. Jesus then asked Zacchaeus, a lowly tax collector, if he, Jesus, could dine with him rather than with the leaders of the town. Appearances and reputation did not cloud Jesus' perception. He saw beyond them to the heart of the person. (Luke 19:1-10) This is of the essence of wisdom.

Wisdom of Other Traditions

Another illustration of the way of wisdom is found in the life of the Buddha, the Enlightened One. Oriental art presents us with many pictures of the Buddha. He is represented as a man of wisdom or of compassion or of both. This spirit is well illustrated in a story told of his attitude toward many speculative questions he was asked.

A disciple of the Buddha once wondered if the world was eternal or not eternal. He asked the Buddha to enlighten him. The Buddha responded with the following parable:

It is as if a man had been wounded by an arrow thickly smeared with poison and his friends and companions, his relatives and kinsfolk, were to procure for him a physician or surgeon; and the sick man were to say: "I will not have this arrow taken out until I have learnt whether the man who wounded me belonged to the warrior caste, or to the Brahmin caste, or to the agricultural caste, or to the menial caste."

Or again he were to say, "I will not have this arrow taken out until I have learnt the name of the man who wounded me, and to what clan he belongs."

Or again he were to say, "I will not have this arrow taken out until I have learned whether the man who wounded me was tall, or short, or of the middle height."

Or again he were to say, "I will not have this arrow taken out until I have learnt whether the man who wounded me was black, or dusky, or of a yellow skin. . . . "

That man would die without ever having learnt the answers to his questions.

In exactly the same way anyone who should say, "I will not follow the Buddha until he explains to me either that the world is eternal or that the world is not eternal," that person would die.

For whether the world is eternal or not eternal, there still remain birth, old age, death, sorrow, lamentation, misery, grief, and despair. My concern is the cure of these maladies.[2]

The questions to which the Buddha will respond, the concerns for which he will show a care, are those that arise from the very life of the person. The Buddha is filled with a compassion for the suffering person. He has an eye for that which is truly suffering and that which is truly a cure. This is wisdom.

A third example of a wise person is found in the founder of Hasidism, the Baal-Shem-Tov, the Master of the Good Name of God. The following story shows the spirit of this wise Jewish man. It speaks not only of his wisdom but also of a way to discern whether a person is wise or not:

> The disciples of the Baal-Shem heard that a certain man had a great reputation for learning. Some of them wanted to go to him and find out what he had to teach. The master gave them permission to go, but first they asked him: "And how shall we be able to tell whether he is a true zaddik (wise person)?" The Baal-Shem replied: "Ask him to advise you what to do to keep unholy thoughts from disturbing you in your prayers and studies. If he gives you advice, then you will know that he belongs to those who are of no account. For this is the service of men in the world to the very hour of their death; to struggle time after time with the extraneous, and time after time to uplift and fit it into the nature of the Divine Name."[3]

This is wisdom, to see into the heart of the everyday, each day. It is not necessarily a single answer. Nor does it mean a different answer all the time. Rather, it is to meet the everyday, to struggle with it and, seeing into its heart, to uplift it and to be uplifted.

Wisdom and Prayer

Wisdom often arises out of a question and leads to another question which probes the life of the inquirer. Wisdom gathers what is scattered as it scatters what is thought to be gathered. It is deeply compassionate and leads to wonder and silence. It is expressive of a sage's intrinsic relatedness to a particular situation, yet places that unique event in the context of mystery. To be wise is to see things as they are. And this is prayer. Finally, wisdom is a gift. It is grace. Saint Paul speaks of this gift when he writes:

> How rich are the depths of God — how deep his wisdom and knowledge — and how impossible to penetrate his motives or understand his methods! *Who could ever know the mind of the Lord? . . . Who could ever give him anything or lend him anything?* All that exists comes from him; all is by him and for him. To him be glory for ever! Amen. (Romans 11:33-36)

To pray is to search out the mind of God in the midst of existence, in the midst of our questionings and wonderings and silences. To pray is to seek out the mystery in the heart of life, to see things as they are, to be perceptive in the midst of our relations. To pray involves a seeing into the heart of life, with compassion and understanding, knowledge and love. It does not shrink from action but acts when action is called for, and remains quiet when quiet is demanded. To pray is to live while we live and to die while we die!

Notes

1. Elie Wiesel, *The Town Beyond the Wall* (New York: Avon, 1969), p. 118.
2. E. A. Burtt, ed., *The Teachings of the Compassionate Buddha* (New York: Mentor, 1955), pp. 34-35.
3. Martin Buber, *Tales of the Hasidim: The Early Masters* (New York: Schocken, 1947), p. 66.

Conclusion

These pages have been about prayer. Many times it might have seemed that I had wandered away from my subject. Traditionally, prayer has been spoken of as prayer of petition, praise, thanksgiving, and reparation. It has been described as contemplation. I have not used this language because I believe that it can be misleading. It is a language that often relegates prayer to a chapel or to a formalized setting. This formal prayer — whether it is in written forms or whether it is spoken in one's own words, whether it is in the quiet of one's room or chapel or whether it is shared prayer — is not exactly what I have been speaking of. It is not excluded. But it is seen to be too narrow a description. What I have been trying to uncover are various experiences that are at the root of such prayer and to which such prayer can lead. My thesis is that participation in such root experiences is itself prayerful.

It is my experience that prayer happens in the day-to-day and that the formulations we generally associate with prayer are expressions of various dimensions of this everyday. As I see it, that everyday is a cosmotheandric network of relations, a network in which three dimensions are intricately woven: the divine, the human, and the cosmic. Within this network, we question and wonder and are silent. We try to see our relations in this network as clearly as possible, with sensitivity and awareness and compassion. We, in a word, seek wisdom, the flavor of life at the heart of life. To be engaged in these experiences is to pray.

The very fiber of life is prayer. While we may learn to pray at a time and in a place, prayer happens at no special time, in no special place. Prayer is grace. Its limits are the boundaries of human existence itself, boundaries which can be described as mystery, the ''evermore'' of life.

Where is that mystery? Right here, right now. And we can see and hear and touch it with our bodies and our minds and our hearts. Yet, at the same time it can be missed. I will conclude with some free verse which gives expression to my experience of prayer, an experience which itself sometimes touches the heart and sometimes misses.

Prayer?

To enter a dark room
The sun has shone here
It is warm
I do not know the sun
It is here — I know
I know it not

To be in a dark room
Reaching for walls that
never appear
I do not know them
They are here — I know
I know them not

To serve in a dark room
To love in a dark room
To open my eyes in a dark room
To pain in a dark room

To be available in a dark room
To be tired in a dark room
To be controlled in a dark room
To control in a dark room
To be alienated in a dark room
To be finite in a dark room
To be scared in a dark room
To rejoice in a dark room
To listen in a dark room
To work in a dark room
To see in a dark room
To walk in a dark room
To stumble in a dark room
To fall in a dark room
To sleep in a dark room
To get up in a dark room

To ask nothing
To receive nothing
To possess nothing

To ask everything
To receive everything
To possess everything

Sometimes . . .